GW00391862

Napoleon and Europe

Philip Ingram

Series Historical Consultant:
Dr R. A. H. Robinson,
The University of Birmingham

Stanley Thornes (Publishers) Ltd

First published in 1998 by:
Stanley Thornes (Publishers) Ltd,
Ellenborough House,
Wellington Street,
CHELTENHAM GL50 1YW
England

98 99 00 01 02 / 10 9 8 7 6 5 4 3 2 1

A catalogue record for this book is available from the British Library.

ISBN 0 7487 3954 8

Cover photograph from the National Gallery Picture Library

Illustrated by Hardlines, Charlbury, Oxfordshire and Oxford Illustrators Ltd

Typeset by Tech-Set Ltd, Gateshead, Tyne and Wear

Printed and bound in Great Britain by Redwood Books, Trowbridge, Wiltshire

Acknowledgements

With thanks to the following for permission to reproduce photographs in this book:

Bibliothèque Nationale, Paris/Bulloz/Bridgeman Art Library: p.34, The Imperial Family of France (engraving) by French School (19th century): p.43, Long live the Emperor!, March 23rd, 1815 (engraving) by French School (19th century); Collection Malmaison, p.63; Dome des Invalides, Paris/Bulloz/Bridgeman Art Library: p.48, The Tomb of Napoleon Bonaparte; Fotomas Index, p.17; Louvre, Paris/Giraudon/ Bridgeman Art Library: p.6, The Consecration of the Emperor Napoleon and Coronation of the Empress Josephine, 2nd December, 1804, detail from the central panel, 1806–7 by Jacques Louis David (1748–1825); Mary Evans Picture Library, p.46; Musée Condé, Chantilly/Giraudon/Bridgeman Art Library: p.47, The Triumph of the Consul Bonaparte (post restoration) (pencil on paper) by Pierre-Paul Prud'hon (1758–1823); Musée Nationale de la Légion d'Honneur, Paris/Bulloz/Bridgeman Art Library: p.21, The First Distribution of Crosses of the Legion of Honour in the Church of the Invalides, 1812, detail, (oil on canvas) by Jean Baptiste Debret (1768–1848); National Army Museum, p.45; Prado, Madrid/Index/Bridgeman Art Library: p.39, Execution of the Defenders of Madrid, 3rd May, 1808, by Francisco José de Goya y Lucientes (1746–1828), 1814.

Every effort has been made to contact copyright holders. The publishers apologise to anyone whose rights have been inadvertently overlooked, and will be happy to rectify any errors or omissions.

For Mabel and Arthur, who are always there

Contents

How to Use this Book

History at A-level is a more complex and demanding subject than at any preceding level, and it is with these new and higher demands on students in mind that the Pathfinder History series has been written. The basic aim of the book is simple: to enable you to appreciate the important issues that lie behind Napoleon's rule in France and Europe, how he triumphed and how he was overthrown.

What this book does not do is provide a single source of all the answers needed for exam success. The very nature of A-level study demands that you use a range of resources in your studies, in order to build up the understanding of different interpretations on issues, and develop your own argument on exam topics. Pathfinder can make this subject more accessible by defining the key issues, giving an initial understanding of them and helping you to define questions for further investigation. It concentrates on the fund-amentals surrounding Napoleon's impact on history; the important issues, events and other characters of his period that you must understand, and which the examiners will want to see that you know.

Hence it becomes more of a guide book to the subject, and can be used whenever you want within the A-level course; as an introduction, as a reminder revision text or throughout the course each time a new topic is started. Pathfinder also has several important features to help you get to grips with Napoleon and his times.

The book follows the three basic stages of the A-level process, explaining why they are important and why you are doing them. The three sections of the book are thus Overview, Enquiry and Investigation, and Review. These describe the three main methods of studying History at A-level; so, for example, when you answer a question on the background to Napoleon's downfall, you will recall why this book approaches this topic with these three headings in mind.

KEY ISSUES AND KEY SKILLS

Pathfinder is written around three basic principles. The first is that it covers the most important events, themes, ideas and concepts of the subject, called the *Key Issues*. The second is that there are levels or tiers to these issues, so that a major question is broken down into its contributory questions and issues and is thus easier to understand. And the third principle is that there are fundamental skills that you must develop and employ as historians at this level, and these are referred to as the *Key Skills*.

These principles combine in Section 1, where **The Big Picture** sets the whole scene of the topic, and identifies the most important periods and events within the topic. What **The Key Issues** does is to establish what the author believes are the fundamental questions and answers to the subject as a whole, and then examine these in more detail by raising contributory questions contained within the main question. Each period is discussed in more detail in Section 2, and you will see page references for each appropriate chapter. Each period thus has its own issues and concepts, to provide a second tier of Key Issues. Finally, the **What to Read, how to Read, where to Find it and how to Use it** section offers hints and advice on the active study skills you will be using in A-level History.

The main focus of the book is Section 2, called **Enquiry and Investigation** because this is exactly what you are being asked to do for most of the time during the A-level process. You are making historical enquiries and learning how to interpret sources and information every time you look at a document, analyse a photograph or read around a topic. Each chapter takes as its title one of the periods identified in The Big Picture, and each one also identifies what you need to bear in mind when working on that particular issue or theme.

There is a useful little tab at the start of each spread which summarises the most important aspects of the topic and identifies the skills that you will need to use when studying it. These are the Key Skills, although you could think of them as key study skills if you prefer. There are a number of them and they can be grouped together in the following headings with these definitions:

Skills for collecting information from historical sources

- Analysis: breaking down information into component parts (making notes under section headings, for example).
- Interpretation: considering the implications of information and cross-referencing to other sources or contextual knowledge to develop your understanding further. (Skills used within this are actually inference, deduction, extrapolation, interpolation, recall and synthesis.)
- Evaluation: assessing the validity of sources and hence the implications for the reliability of the information that they provide.
- Recording: arranging information into sections that allow easy retrieval when required. For example, making linear notes (good for large amounts of information), diagrams and flow-charts or mind maps (good for establishing relationships between sections of information).

Skills for applying and using information

- Explanation: using information to show how and why something happened.
- Assessment: weighing up possible explanations or interpretations.
- Forming hypotheses: setting up an explanation or judgement for further testing.
- Testing hypotheses: using information to support and challenge a hypothesis to improve it.
- Setting a thesis: using the information to present, support and sustain a tested hypothesis and an explanation of historical processes.

You will see that some are flagged more often than others, and there may be others, such as chronology, that are not defined here. However, the important point to remember is that these are the skills that the A-level historian has to have available for use, and that you are actually using them all the time already. The aim is to reinforce these skills for you, and to enable you to see how you are using them and why.

Section 3 **Review** then brings all the interpretations, investigations and issues that you have looked at on Napoleon into one place. **Synthesis** is the bringing together of issues, arguments and judgements into overall answers. It also poses answers as to what the author considers to be the main issues identified in Section 1. **Argument** then takes the information and hypotheses and applies them to more detailed essay answers, of the style you might find or that you might write in the exam. The **Final Review** is something of the author's own thoughts and conclusions to the subject on a broad level.

MARGINS AND ICONS

Pathfinder divides material as part of the main aim of focusing attention on the most important issues. Hence the main central narrative discusses and interprets information and, although detailed, cannot provide all the information on its topic. It can be integrated with and supplemented by more detailed books, articles and documents.

All other sorts of information appear in the margins and you will see the following icons used alongside them. Not all icons appear in every chapter and some chapters have other features included as well, but the icons should help you manage the extra information given on topics.

 Documents, historiography and sources – quotes from texts, individuals and passages

 Suggested headings for notes

 Suggested further reading

 Sample activities and exam-style questions

 General hints, study tips and advice

 Key terms

This book is a biography of one exceptional man who, in a short life lasting 51 years, managed to rise from complete obscurity, first of all to become dictator of France, then to rule much of Europe, and finally to challenge for world domination.

It is history on many levels. It is the story of one individual and the factors that allowed him to gain so much power; but such is the legacy of Napoleon that his story is also the history of both France and Europe.

The next four pages provide you with a brief account of the life of Napoleon and his impact on France and Europe. Each titled section on these pages is a summary of a chapter from Section 2 of the book. Together they will give you an overview, or the Big Picture.

Don't worry ... you don't have to remember all this right away. This is just an introduction to the book and the period. It aims to set what you are going to learn in context. By starting here you should be able to get an overview and see how all the chapters of the book fit together into a whole. There are other ways of using this chapter:

- You can refer back to each section here after you have read the full chapters. This will help you to fix the most important points of each chapter in your mind.
- If you wish to read a later chapter without having to start at the beginning, you might put your reading in context by referring to the summary sections that cover the previous chapters.
- You should find this chapter especially useful for revision when you have finished the book.

The Big Picture: Napoleon and Europe

'The Coronation' by Jacques-Louis David, a massive work suggesting the grandeur of the Empire. Several people who disapproved of Napoleon's coronation and refused to attend were deliberately included in the picture.

NAPOLEON'S RISE TO POWER 1769–1799 (see pages 14–17)

- Napoleon's relatively humble origins as a minor noble on the island of Corsica meant that he was fortunate to get an education on mainland France and then an officer's commission in the Royal Army.
- The Revolution provided vacancies in the officer corps and gave Napoleon the opportunity to prove himself. He won promotion at the siege of Toulon and helped put down a royalist rising in Paris.
- He commanded an army which defeated the Austrians and Piedmontese in Italy during 1796–1797. He negotiated the peace treaty of Campo Formio.
- In 1798 he led an expedition to Egypt which, although it ultimately failed, added to his image in France as a military saviour.
- When he returned from Egypt he exploited weakness and division in the Directory to seize power in the Coup de Brumaire.

FROM CONSULATE TO EMPIRE 1799–1804 (see pages 18–21)

- Napoleon installed a constitution which gave him enormous power as First Consul. The elections were rigged and those who were elected had no power.
- He had the power to appoint local officials and he used this to put his supporters in place all over the country. Propaganda, censorship and a system of police spies were used to increase his control over the state.
- His position was made much more secure by his victory over Austria at Marengo. This led to a general European peace by 1802, which allowed him to concentrate on domestic government and make himself First Consul for life.
- Despite many royalist plots against him, he tried to pacify the royalists with concessions. He dealt very harshly with the extreme republicans (Jacobins) who also opposed him.
- By 1804 he had used a system of rewards and punishments to create a body of administrators from all political and social backgrounds which helped him keep power. He declared himself Emperor of France.

NAPOLEON AND FRANCE 1800–1804 (see pages 22–25)

- In 1801 he ended a quarrel between revolutionary France and the Pope by signing the Concordat. He hoped that this would make the Catholic church support him.
- The economy was stabilised by setting up the Bank of France to regulate money supply and to control inflation. Government finances were improved by reforms to the tax system.
- Chaos in the legal system was ended by the codification of the laws under the Civil Code (later called the Code Napoléon). Privilege was abolished but some of the new laws were very authoritarian, particularly towards women and workers.
- Limited reform of education took place. *Lycées* were set up to train students for future state service. Church schools also prospered, but the education of women and of the poor was completely neglected.

THE CONQUEST OF EUROPE 1805–1807 (see pages 26–29)

- Napoleon went to war against a Third Coalition of enemies in 1805. He defeated Austria at Ulm and then crushed an Austro-Russian army at Austerlitz.
- Any hopes that he may have had of invading Britain were dashed by the destruction of the French fleet at Trafalgar.

Some of the words in the text will be completely new to you. Have a look at this list. It will explain the most obscure ones.

Directory – the republican government which ruled France between 1795 and 1799

Coup – an armed seizure of power

Brumaire – the month in which Napoleon seized power (according to the new calendar introduced by the revolutionaries)

Consulate – the period (1799–1804) before the Empire when Napoleon was ruler but France was still a republic

Constitution – a document that sets out the responsibilities and limitations of government power

Concordat – an agreement signed by Napoleon and the Pope which clarified the position of the Catholic church in France

Privilege – a situation where certain groups, e.g. the nobility or the church, gain preferential consideration in politics, law, taxation etc.

Lycée – a special state school set up by Napoleon

Coalition – an alliance. During the revolutionary and Napoleonic Wars, four coalitions fought against France. The First Coalition (1792–1797) was effectively ended by Napoleon's victories over Austria in 1797. The Second Coalition (1798–1801) was ended by French victories at Marengo and Hohenlinden. The Third Coalition (1805–1807) ended at Tilsit, while the Fourth Coalition (1813–1814) defeated and overthrew Napoleon in 1814.

Why study Napoleon?

It may seem to you that it would be more relevant to study recent history. After all, the world we inhabit is much closer to Hitler and Roosevelt than it is to the pre-industrial age of Napoleon, and, if you are to make sense of the world today, you need to understand twentieth-century terms like dictatorship, totalitarianism, democracy and communism.

Napoleon nevertheless remains highly relevant to the creation of the modern world. His life spans the divide between a Europe ruled by hereditary kings who said they were divinely appointed and our own world of democracies and dictators who claim power by popular will.

Existing as he did in a time of great contrast and change, Napoleon presents us with a real conundrum. To whom are we to compare him? An emperor from ancient Rome or a modern dictator like Hitler? Was the empire that he created modern or ancient? And did it foreshadow a future which has yet to happen – a United States of Europe?

However long ago Napoleon lived, the reforms that he introduced to France and spread across Europe still live with us today. Legal equality, state education and the removal of religion from government all shape our own lives. Unfortunately, Napoleon's dark side also provides a template for the brutality of modern regimes. His secret police, spies, propaganda, censorship, arrests and executions are still a fact of life in many parts of the world.

The study of Napoleon at his best and at his worst helps us to understand our own world.

- Prussia declared war in 1806 but was badly beaten at the battles of Jena and Auerstadt and eventually had to sign a very harsh peace treaty.
- Russia was beaten at Friedland in 1807 and Tsar Alexander made an alliance with Napoleon at Tilsit.
- The allies had incompetent commanders, poor plans, outmoded tactics and poor coordination. Napoleon had a united command and a clear purpose. His army and his plans were far superior to those of his enemies.
- Napoleon launched the Continental System in a bid to defeat Britain by closing all European ports to British trade. He hoped to bankrupt the country.

NAPOLEONIC WARFARE (see pages 30–33)

- During the Revolution major changes to the nature of warfare occurred and made France militarily far superior to other European states which continued to use older, less effective techniques.
- Napoleon invented no new techniques but he benefited greatly from the changes brought about by the Revolution.
- Historians dispute whether he was a military genius because he made many mistakes, particularly later in his career when his army declined in quality and he grew tired and sick.
- His main strengths include his detailed planning, flexibility and opportunism, and his great ability to inspire the soldiers under his command and to intimidate enemy commanders.
- After their defeats of 1805–1807 his enemies reformed their military and adopted new techniques which made them much more formidable.

NAPOLEON'S EUROPE 1805–1813 (see pages 34–37)

- The Empire consisted of satellites ruled by his relatives and allied states where the old rulers were allowed to keep their thrones.
- Napoleon later claimed that he wanted a Europe which would be a federation of free nation states, but he centralised all power on himself and gave the peoples of his Empire no independence.
- Most areas witnessed some reform, but this was patchy and was really aimed at making the territories of the Empire more efficient and productive of money and manpower to fight Napoleon's wars.
- Europe was ruthlessly exploited so as to cushion the effect of the wars on France. Many states were driven to bankruptcy.
- Popular opposition to French rule was largely muted and passive (with the exception of Spain). It tended to focus on loyalty to the old dynasties, religion and tradition, and was rarely liberal or nationalist in the modern sense.

Reactionary – a person who wishes to revert to an out-of-date political or social system

THE DOWNFALL OF NAPOLEON 1807–1814
(see pages 38–41)

- The Continental System had little effect on Britain and Napoleon's high-handed methods of enforcement made him many enemies in Europe. It also led him to war in Spain (1808) and Russia (1812).
- The war in Spain and Portugal was very expensive and dragged on for six years, forcing Napoleon to divide his resources on two fronts. In Spain the French had to fight thousands of guerrillas as well as a British army under the Duke of Wellington.
- Austria declared war on him in 1809, and although they were eventually beaten at Wagram they fought so well that Napoleon sought an alliance with the Habsburgs through marriage.
- A huge army was destroyed in Russia and this gave his enemies a chance to combine and attack him while he was weak. He was beaten at Leipzig by the Fourth Coalition in 1813.
- The Fourth Coalition invaded France and he was forced to abdicate and retire to Elba in 1814.

THE HUNDRED DAYS 1815 (see pages 42–45)

- Napoleon was very unhappy on Elba. He feared rumours that he was to be sent further away from France and was worried by the refusal of the Bourbons to pay his pension.
- Encouraged by stories of divisions among the allies and discontent in France, he returned to the mainland and rallied the army to him.
- In order to win domestic support he issued the 'Additional Act' which liberalised the old Napoleonic constitution.
- He attempted to negotiate a peace, but the allies declared him an outlaw and set about mobilising huge armies to depose him.
- Napoleon struck first by marching into Belgium to confront the British and Prussians. He was beaten at Waterloo and sent into exile on the island of St Helena.

NAPOLEON: THE LEGEND (see pages 46–49)

- During his time in power Napoleon had always been keen to leave behind an image of himself as a great soldier and a wise statesman.
- During his last years on St Helena he spent his time dictating to his companions in exile. Their accounts show how Napoleon attempted to justify his life and portray himself as a martyr, unjustly punished by the reactionary European powers.
- His image-making efforts were successful and have made it difficult for subsequent historians to establish a 'real' Napoleon from the myth that he created.
- Today many historians are still questioning the truth of Napoleon's self-created legend as a political liberal, a liberator of oppressed European peoples and a military genius.

'Key Issues' give the study of history a purpose. Without them history is merely a story. They are the 'why' and the 'how' of history, rather than just the 'what'.

As you know, the study of A-level History is about much more than learning what happened. At GCSE you should have learnt that, in addition to describing facts and chronology, you must use evidence and explain different interpretations of events. Elsewhere in this book you will find that you need to investigate, analyse and assess historical events in order to achieve success at A-level.

The 'Key Issues' are the questions that you should ask yourself when studying history. It is all too easy sometimes to read about history but not really understand it. Textbooks too often tell you things without showing you their importance or why they happened in the first place, and leave you wondering why any specific event is in the text. This can be very frustrating and often leaves you with an incomplete understanding of the subject.

A real understanding of history comes from being able to identify the crucial areas and ask the important questions. This is the purpose of the 'Key Issues'. As you work your way through the text you will find that there is a 'Key Issues' section on each spread. These are designed to help you ask all the questions that are important for each topic. By asking them, and keeping them in mind as you work through the chapters, you should reach a deeper understanding of the subject.

'Key Issues' are the building blocks for the sort of essays you will get in A-level examinations. If you understand them and have retained a good level of knowledge, you can consider yourself well prepared.

The Key Issues

1. DID NAPOLEON BETRAY THE REVOLUTION?

The impact of the Revolution and Napoleon's subsequent rule on France must never be underestimated. During the years 1800–1804 Napoleon established a system of government which was to some extent influenced by the Revolution, and which was to be transplanted throughout Europe.

What debt did Napoleon owe to the Revolution for his ideas on domestic government? Was he faithful to the spirit of the Revolution or did he cynically subvert it for his own authoritarian ends? Did Napoleon give France equality, individual liberty and representative government? Was the order and stability that he established really brought about at the cost of dictatorship? Did he genuinely care about the ideals of the Revolution, or were his more liberal measures merely about pacifying public opinion?

Is his collaboration with elements of the *ancien régime* (old regime), such as the church and the nobility, evidence of his contempt for the Revolution, or does it show a simple desire to end its excesses? Was his education policy really about making careers open to talent? Is the Code Napoléon a revolutionary or an authoritarian document? Is there any evidence for his claim that he represented 'popular sovereignty'?

2. WHY WAS NAPOLEON ABLE TO CONQUER EUROPE?

Napoleon's conquest of Europe between 1805 and 1807 led to enormous political and social changes throughout the continent which were to influence the entire history of the nineteenth century. It is therefore very important that we understand how it was that one state could defeat so many others in such a short space of time.

At the centre of the issue are the individuals involved. How significant was Napoleon's ability as a military commander? Why was his form of diplomacy so effective? Why were allied commanders unable to match him? And why were they so hopelessly divided?

Beyond the individuals lie much larger factors, such as the nature of the competing armies, states and societies. Does the superiority of the French military provide an adequate explanation of allied defeats? To what extent was that superiority the result of political and social advantages enjoyed by France which the allies could not hope to match? Given their advantages, was the French victory inevitable?

Lastly, how do we compare the relative importance of individuals with the significance of the larger social, political and military factors? Was the triumph of the French really down to the genius of Napoleon, or did he merely exploit many other factors which he neither originated nor controlled?

3. WHAT BROUGHT ABOUT NAPOLEON'S DOWNFALL?

Napoleon's dominance of Europe was brief, but almost complete. Within seven years he went from master of Europe to monarch of Elba. How do we account for the suddenness of his downfall? Even Napoleon later admitted that he made mistakes, but can we say that one of these errors was more important than all the others? Do we trace his decline to his hatred of Britain and his Continental System, his occupation of Spain, or his invasion of Russia?

Can the reasons for his downfall be expressed in purely military terms? Did his ability as a commander undergo relative decline after 1807? Was the changing quality of the Grand Army a significant factor? When did his situation really become hopeless? Was he irretrievably beaten by 1813? If France had rallied to him against the invaders of the Fourth Coalition, could he have reversed his defeats in 1814?

Does the real fault lie with Napoleon himself, or should we look to the positive action of his many enemies? Was his downfall brought about by monarchs, generals, governments and armies, or was it down to the peoples of Europe who reacted against French oppression and took up arms to assert their own national identity or to protect their traditional society?

4. NAPOLEON'S EUROPE: LIBERATION OR EXPLOITATION?

Despite its short existence, the Empire made an impact on the lives of millions of people outside France, and therefore must have had some effect on the subsequent history of Europe. What were Napoleon's intentions for his enormous empire? Did he ultimately aim to create one united superstate, or did he want a federation of equal nation states? Did he hope to spread the liberal gains of the Revolution across Europe, or was his goal simply to exploit the continent for the benefit of France? Was the Empire in any way a deliberate and pre-planned creation, or was it simply brought about by a series of military and strategic necessities? Is there a uniform pattern of change in the areas dominated by France? To what extent was the Empire guided by any principle? Did it consider the welfare and wishes of its subjects?

What were the real effects of French conquest on the people of Europe? Who benefited and who suffered? And how deep did the social and political change brought about by French victories really go? Which groups were willing to collaborate with Napoleon and why? How and why did Napoleon exploit Europe for the benefit of France? Why was there so little popular resistance against French rule and what form did this resistance take?

History is everywhere!

While writing this book, I pulled a Christmas cracker. The joke inside read, 'Where did Napoleon keep his armies?' Answer: 'Up his sleevies!' This story illustrates my point. History is everywhere!

Historical information used to mean only one thing: the written word. The job of historians was to delve into reams of written evidence in the form of diaries, letters and documents, and to emerge with their findings to be presented in books, magazines and monographs.

Today historians have come to realise that a historical source consists of much more than what is written – it is the whole range of artifacts left from the past. Buildings and monuments are now read like books. Paintings and sculptures reveal people's political and cultural aspirations. Music puts us in touch with past emotions, and even something as intangible as folk-memory is recorded and studied by academics.

Some of these sources may not be relevant to the study of Napoleon, but you should make the deliberate effort to understand the man and his time through more than textbooks. In the case of Napoleon, artworks are of particular value. Throughout this text there are images of Napoleon, usually presented in the way he chose. What do they say about him? Delve into the arts or the oversized book section of your library and find some of them enlarged and in colour.

If you want to get close to him, you could try the available primary sources. His published memoirs only cover the period up to Marengo and then jump to the Hundred Days. They are full of self-justification. Much more satisfactory are his letters which give a great and sensitive insight into the man and his work.

What to Read, how to Read, where to Find it and how to Use it

1. WHERE TO FIND INFORMATION

The obvious starting point for your study of Napoleon is this book. But at 64 pages long this book is not, nor is it meant to be, comprehensive. Its aim is to provide you with an informed starting point. For a thorough understanding you must be willing to look elsewhere. Start by asking your teacher, and check out the available resources within the History department and the school library. After that, you will need to use a public library. A good library will have some books on Napoleon but it probably will not have exactly what you are looking for. In this case you should ask at the desk and be prepared to place an order for any book that they don't have. For a small charge the library will 'borrow' books from other libraries. This is a process that usually takes a couple of weeks, so you must plan ahead and be prepared to wait.

Most libraries divide their stock into topic sections all listed under a numerical code known as the Dewey system. To find out if they have any books on Napoleon simply follow the numbers around the shelves until you get to 944.05. As well as the normal borrowing section, most libraries will also have a section for oversized books. This may be especially useful if you want to find books with large and lavish illustrations. You might also try the reference section of the library.

2. ACTIVE INFORMATION-SEEKING

All historians have a duty to examine any issue using a range of different sources in order to ensure a balanced judgement. You are no different. You must use other books. Many of the books that you might use for A-level are seriously thick tomes and, if you're being realistic, you won't have time to read them. That's why it's so important to read selectively. Don't grab any old book that happens to be about Napoleon – some books are of much more value than others. Get the most up-to-date text that you can and read through the Bibliography at the end. Many new books actually contain a bibliographical essay which will guide you around the available scholarship and enable you to select the most relevant and up-to-date books possible.

Don't attempt to read every page of every book. Read selectively. If you're working on a specific area (for example, Napoleon as a military commander), then use the chapter headings. If you want to know about something more specific, such as the Battle of Austerlitz, look it up in the index at the back of the book. In general it is useful to start with a fairly broad-ranging book to provide a framework, which then allows you to be increasingly selective. This book is one attempt to provide such a framework.

3. NOTE-TAKING

You should make notes in the way that you feel suits you best. Some people prefer to make notes in a traditional way, with titles, sub-titles, paragraphs and sentences. If this is what you want to do, then you can use the titles in each chapter to provide a structure for your notes.

Most chapters in this book include sections in the margin intended to help you with note-taking. Many include diagrams which should provide you with a concise and easy aid for revision. More than that, the diagrams have been designed to enable you to answer the questions in the 'Activities' sections. These activities have been created to help you to test your understanding of the Key Issues.

This form of note-taking is particularly useful for detailed information about a particular topic. The use of flow-charts and diagrams helps to summarise relationships and links between topics and factors.

If you do choose to use the diagrams and lists suggested in the text, then don't be afraid to change or add to them when you think it is useful. Refer to other books to broaden the depth of the information in your diagrams. If one side of A4 is too small for the information you wish to record, then split your diagram sections into whole pages with a key diagram as an overall guide to your notes. Pin the pages up on the wall and see how thorough an answer you can provide.

Notes initially generate questions for you, but one of the main tests is whether they actually help you to answer a question. Therefore, complete at least one of the diagrams and attempt the activity that follows it. You might be surprised at how well it works!

4. PERSONAL ORGANISATION

History A-level is only a part of your life and it's probably only a part of your studies, so it's essential that you organise your time properly in order to achieve a balance.

The best idea is to draw up a study timetable and stick to it. Don't 'binge' on one particular topic at the expense of others, and don't leave work untouched until a looming deadline forces you to rush it – with very unsatisfactory results. This 'stop–go' approach will not help you achieve your full potential, and it will add to the stress of A-level exams. Sit down, work out your priorities, and apportion your available time in order to meet all your needs.

Make sure that you set a time limit on your History sessions. If they are too long, you will not feel the full benefit. Up to two hours at a time is about right. However, concentration is a skill that needs to be learnt and practised like most others. You could start with, say, an hour, and then have a break. Make it more interesting for yourself by varying the activity between note-taking, essay-writing, reading, using technology and watching videos. Don't be afraid to 'study around' the subject occasionally in order to satisfy your own personal interest. Above all, enjoy it. History's the best!

Technology

Modern technology is a vital new aid in the study of history. Commercially produced videos on Napoleon exist, and there are a range of films including the 1970 feature film *Waterloo*. Otherwise it pays to keep a careful eye on the TV listings. They sometimes provide a good support for your course of study.

Information technology is also increasingly significant. The Internet is packed with references to Napoleon, although it may take you some time to find anything of specific value. At the time of writing there is at least one CD-Rom dealing solely with Napoleon, and this number is set to increase as the technology itself becomes more widespread.

Your greatest resource

If you are in a class studying A-level, then you and your classmates must realise that the greatest resource you have is each other. Remember that you are not competing against each other – you are trying to get the best mark you can. If you do help someone else, it will do you no harm. If someone writes a good essay or some handy notes, or if they find a particularly useful text, they should share it. Each student should photocopy their best essay for the rest of the group when you near the exam. That way, everybody benefits. You must always remember, however, that sharing is not a one-way process. It is not an excuse for someone to avoid work and live off the effort of others. Everyone must contribute to the best of their ability. Sharing is also very different from copying.

THE KEY ISSUE

- What factors and events helped Napoleon's rise as a soldier?

THE KEY SKILLS

Chronology
Assessment
Explanation

Historical background

Under the *ancien régime* France was ruled by the Bourbon monarchy. Louis XVI appeared all-powerful, but his country was in decline and he faced a worsening financial crisis.

In 1789 a revolution in Paris forced him to share power with an elected Constituent Assembly. Louis could not work with the Assembly. He plotted with foreign monarchies against the Revolution and this led France into war with the First Coalition led by Austria and Prussia. Within France he was overthrown and eventually executed.

In the first year war went badly and the situation only improved when the extremist Jacobin party seized power and used harsh measures known as the Terror. Their methods led to a virtual civil war in France which was put down with great brutality. Some Frenchmen supported the invaders. Toulon welcomed the enemy and had to be taken by French troops.

The war began to go well and the Jacobins were overthrown by more moderate republicans. A new government called the Directory took power. They managed to defeat a royalist uprising in Paris, but more military defeats meant that France was threatened by a growing number of foreign enemies.

Napoleon's Growing Popularity

EARLY LIFE 1769–1793

Napoleon was born on Corsica in 1769. This poor and backward island was more Italian than French, having been ceded by Genoa to France in 1768. Its people held fierce family loyalties rather like the clans of highland Scotland. Napoleon was the second son of a minor nobleman. This, together with his mother's friendship with Corsica's French governor, enabled him to gain an education in mainland France at government expense.

At school in Brienne, and later at the Ecole Militaire in Paris where he trained in the artillery, the young Napoleon was an outsider, standing out from most of the other students by his Italian accent. In 1785 he became a junior officer in the artillery, but his relatively low social status meant that he was unlikely to rise to a more senior rank.

1789

1792

The Revolution, however, transformed his prospects. Many vacancies arose in the higher grades as nobles, refusing to serve the new government, left the army or fled the country altogether. When war broke out, the path to rapid promotion opened up to a whole generation of young French soldiers.

NAPOLEON GAINS NATIONAL PROMINENCE

1793

Thanks to a fellow Corsican named Saliceti and his influential connections among the Jacobins, Napoleon was given control of the artillery at the siege of Toulon. His energy and organisational skill soon helped retake the city, and he was rewarded with the rank of Brigadier-General.

1794

With the overthrow of the Jacobins, the establishment of government by a small group of Directors, and the end of the Terror, he found himself in prison as a Jacobin suspect. Fortunately, his case was investigated by Saliceti and he was soon released. To gain further promotion, he had to shake off his reputation as a Jacobin and find new influential friends. The most important of these was Paul Barras, a ruthless politician prominent in the defeat of the Jacobins. Barras was

1795

military governor of Paris when a royalist rising threatened to overthrow the Directory. Napoleon acted quickly to win Barras' gratitude by turning cannon on the royalist crowd in an incident known as the 'Whiff of Grapeshot'.

1796

Rewarded with command of the Army of Italy, Napoleon was able to put into operation his long-nurtured plan for the defeat of the Piedmontese and Austrians by an invasion across the Alps. Before he left for the field, he married the widowed Josephine Beauharnais.

THE FIRST ITALIAN CAMPAIGN

Napoleon arrived to find the troops ready for action, despite being ill-equipped and unpaid for months. Once again his enormous energy and talent for organisation were evident as he quickly solved the supply problems and boosted morale in a series of speeches promising great plunder in Italy. He crossed the Alps and moved with unexpected speed to knock the small Piedmontese army out of the war before Austria could react. The Austrians were defeated at the Battle of Lodi, and Napoleon occupied Milan. After Lodi he became convinced that he was destined to be one of history's great conquerers.

Without Austrian help, all the other small states which made up the Italian peninsula were at the mercy of the French. They were a treasure house waiting to be plundered. As he marched south, Napoleon forced state after state to pay tribute and accept French dominance. By feeding the Paris press with exaggerated tales of his conquests, Napoleon ensured that his domestic popularity rose to new heights.

Finally, he turned north to face the Austrians who had regrouped after their earlier defeat and were anxious to reassert their position in Italy. But, again victorious, Napoleon advanced to within 60 miles (97 km) of Vienna before agreeing an armistice. His status in France increased further when he personally negotiated the Treaty of Campo Formio, which brought much of Italy under French control. Austria gained Venice, but only after ceding the Austrian Netherlands (present-day Belgium) to France.

Returning to Paris, he found the city benefiting from Italian wealth and crowds flocking to see the plundered works of art. While greeted as a military hero, Napoleon also proved himself a wise and forceful statesman through his diplomacy at Campo Formio.

1796

1797

Historical background

The Directory planned a two-pronged offensive against the Austrians. The main thrust would be into Germany, but a diversion would be launched into Italy with the object of holding down Austrian troops and capturing loot which would ease the economic crisis in France.

The attack into Germany was a failure, but Napoleon's Italian campaign was an enormous and unexpected success and actually knocked Austria out of the war.

Josephine Beauharnais (1763–1814)

Belonged to a wealthy family with estates in Martinique. One-time lover of Paul Barras through whom she met and later married Napoleon. Unfaithful in 1798–1799 with a cavalry officer named Charles. Divorced by Napoleon in 1809 because of her failure to bear him a son.

Paul Barras (1755–1829)

First achieved notoriety as a vicious Jacobin representative to the provinces during the Terror. Befriended Napoleon at the siege of Toulon. Later helped overthrow the Jacobins and put down a royalist uprising in Paris with the aid of Napoleon. Became a Director and obtained the command of the Army of Italy for Napoleon. By the time of Brumaire, disowned by Napoleon because of his corrupt reputation. Rumoured to have accepted money to help restore the Bourbons. Retired from politics after 1799.

Jacobins – the extreme republican party
Terror – the harsh measures used by Jacobins (including mass executions) to ensure the loyalty of France against its foreign enemies
Bourbon – the French royal family in power before the Revolution

THE KEY ISSUES

- What factors helped Napoleon into power?
- How much was his rise to power the result of circumstances which he did not control?
- Was his rise to power inevitable?

THE KEY SKILLS

Assessment
Explanation

Emmanuel Joseph Sieyès (1748–1836)

Former priest famous as a pamphleteer during the early Revolution. Moderate republican who survived the Terror by seeking obscurity. Became a Director in 1799 with the intention of creating a more stable and élitist political system. Could not achieve this within existing constitution, therefore began to plot with Napoleon.

A highly romanticised, but readable, version of Napoleon's early life can be found in Vincent Cronin, *Napoleon* (Collins, 1971). *Napoleon Symphony*, a novel by Anthony Burgess (1974), makes fascinating reading.

Napoleon's Seizure of Power

THE EGYPTIAN ADVENTURE

Many of the Directors now viewed Napoleon's popularity as a political threat. He was given command of an army to attack England, but he believed that French naval weakness made this impossible. Instead, he proposed an attack on Egypt to threaten British commercial interests in India and the Far East. The chance to be rid of Napoleon was too good for the Directors to pass up: the necessary troops and ships were quickly assembled in Toulon.

Egypt was conquered quite easily in 1798, but the whole campaign was doomed when the British navy destroyed the French fleet at anchor in Aboukir Bay. This left the French army stranded without hope of supplies or reinforcement. Perhaps realising that defeat was inevitable and keen to avoid the blame, Napoleon decided to leave his army and slip back to France by fast ship. Some of his officers felt abandoned and betrayed, but he had powerful reasons for leaving. A series of military defeats and economic crises had combined to make the Directory's hold on power look fragile, and Napoleon sensed an opportunity for self-advancement. He had also learned of Josephine's flagrant infidelity and was determined to end a scandal which was making him a laughing stock in fashionable Parisian society.

The ultimate failure of the Egyptian campaign was barely noticed by a public blinded by the romance of the adventure. Napoleon remained a popular hero.

WHY WAS THERE A COUP?

Napoleon arrived back in France in 1799 to find that the situation was not as bad as he had thought. Although all the gains made at Campo Formio had been lost, there was no threat of an invasion of French soil. Napoleon was later to claim that when he returned he found the country in chaos, but historians now realise that he exaggerated the problems in order to justify his own seizure of power.

The real reason for the coup lies in the instability of the political system which threatened at any moment either to bring in an extremist Jacobin government or to return the Bourbons to the throne. In order to avoid this, the Director Sieyès planned to rewrite the constitution to give himself and his friends the power permanently to shut out the extremists. To do this, however, he needed the support of the army to overawe the elected deputies in the two chambers, the Council of the Elders and the Council of the Five Hundred.

Sieyès looked around for a general who would carry out the task. There were many ambitious soldiers to chose from. But his first choice was killed in battle and his second refused the offer. It was only then that he approached Napoleon Bonaparte.

WHAT HAPPENED ON 18 BRUMAIRE?

Sieyès and his friends made careful preparations. They worked hard to build support in the Council of Elders and they ensured that their presence would be felt in the Council of the Five Hundred by having Napoleon's brother Lucien elected its President. Next they made Napoleon commander of the Paris garrison with 8 000 troops at his disposal. They then spread a rumour of an imminent Jacobin plot in Paris in order to get the chambers out of the city and into the suburbs where they could be bullied without interference from the populace.

Their plans almost came to nothing because of the failure of Napoleon to play his part properly. He was never a great public speaker, and when he arrived to address the Council of the Elders on 9 December 1799, he stumbled over his speech and could not be heard. Things got worse when he went to the Council of the Five Hundred. There was uproar, and when some of the delegates attacked him with daggers he had to be rescued from the room by his escort of grenadiers. Outside in the gardens the soldiers looked reluctant to clear the chamber. They had no love for the politicians inside, but they weren't sure that they wanted to be the instruments of a coup which might lead to dictatorship. Lucien saved the day when he dramatically flourished his sword and promised to kill Napoleon should he ever threaten French liberty. The soldiers cleared the hall at bayonet point and a new government was proclaimed. Within a few weeks Napoleon had manipulated his allies into giving him enormous power.

Napoleon 'the Corsican crocodile' dissolving the Council of Frogs. A British cartoon showing the Coup de Brumaire.

The role of the army

Don't make the common mistake of assuming that, because Napoleon was a soldier, his coup was an army takeover. As an individual, he did not represent the collective will of the military. In fact he was only one of many ambitious generals. He used the army, but he did not represent it, nor did the army share power in his government. It was an individual dictatorship, not a military junta. His jealous rivals were given no political power, but, as we shall see, they were compensated with honours and gifts.

Draw up the following table which lists the factors that helped Napoleon to power. Then look carefully through the text and record the evidence for each factor. Notice that these factors are about Napoleon. You should also consider other factors when looking for evidence of Napoleon's rise to power.

Factor	Evidence
Military ability	
Self-publicity	
Corsican connections	
Ability to change political allegiance	
Unprincipled ruthlessness	
Luck	
Opportunism	

Using the information in your notes table, decide if Napoleon's rise to power was inevitable. To what extent was his rise to power due to his own ability?

THE KEY ISSUES

- How did Napoleon assert his will over the entire country after Brumaire?
- What measures did he take to disguise his dictatorship?

THE KEY SKILLS

Investigation
Explanation
Analysis

Dictatorship – a political system in which one person has absolute power
Plebiscite – a direct vote by the people on some question of national importance

Napoleon's view on government (1803)

'I haven't been able to understand yet what good there is in opposition. Whatever it may say, its only result is to diminish the prestige of authority in the eyes of the people.'

Napoleon as First Consul

THE NEW CONSTITUTION

Sieyès had hoped to use the coup to produce a constitution which would shut out the extremists and place power in the hands of a small number of men. He also wanted to avoid dictatorship, so he planned to give each man equal powers and to strictly limit his period in office. During the discussions following the coup, however, Napoleon wore down these safeguards against dictatorship. Thus although the new government was to be headed by three Consuls whose term of office was to be restricted to ten years, he made sure that as First Consul it was he who held real power.

Napoleon took control of the entire political machine by claiming the right to appoint all local government officials directly. Thus he created thousands of officials who, owing their place to his patronage, were likely to pledge their loyalty to him personally. In particular he extended central control over the provinces by dividing the country up into a system of Departments administered by Prefects taking their instructions directly from him.

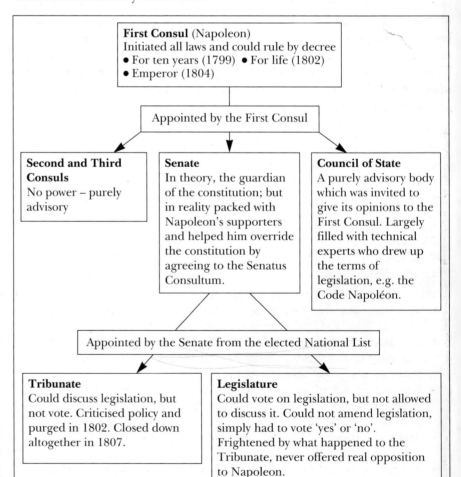

The structure of government under the Consulate

Because he was anxious that his regime should not be compared unfavourably with the ideals of the Revolution, he took great pains to disguise the dictatorship by restoring universal male suffrage and instituting a variety of political assemblies. It was all a sham. The electoral system was so 'indirect' as to exclude any popular choice, and the assemblies were given no power by Napoleon. He generally ignored them and ruled by a decree known as the Senatus Consultum.

PROPAGANDA AND CENSORSHIP

Napoleon now set out to silence the opposition and widen his own appeal. His regime imposed strict press censorship. The majority of Paris newspapers were simply closed down. Those that remained risked closure if they dared to discuss sensitive political issues. For the most part, they had to rely on government reports for their political comment. In the official newspaper *Le Moniteur* these were often written by Napoleon himself. All books had to be approved before publication. Many theatres were closed down. The few that remained open had to obtain government approval before each production.

Meanwhile, Napoleon built up his own image. Government bulletins continued to present a positive message. Accomplished artists such as David, Gros and Ingres won honours and wealth through their portraits of Napoleon as glorious soldier, administrator and statesman. A range of grand public buildings such as the Arc de Triomphe celebrated each victory. Like future dictators, he understood the power of the church and schools in shaping opinion and winning the long-term loyalty of the young (see pages 22–25).

Napoleon often claimed that he represented the will of the people over the selfish and divisive claims of politicians. He would often cite the results of the three plebiscites which he held during the early part of his reign.

Did the plebiscites really show overwhelming support?

Napoleon asked for public approval on:	Yes	No
Brumaire (1799)	3 011 107	1 562
First Consul for Life (1802)	3 600 000	8 374
Empire (1804)	3 572 329	2 569

The results appear conclusive until you consider the following:
- The total electorate has been estimated at between 6 and 8 million. The numbers who did not vote might tell us something about the popular mood.
- In 1799 and 1804 the army's half-million votes were simply added to the 'Yes' total without actually polling the soldiers. They did have a vote in 1802 and 40% of the 'No' votes were polled by soldiers.
- It has been proved that in some areas local officials did not bother to set up a poll – they simply sent in a unanimous 'Yes' vote. In other cases the local officials probably intimidated the electorate.
- Once the figures were in, the Minister of the Interior probably adjusted them to give a much higher 'Yes' vote.
- In each case the plebiscites were held after the decision had been taken – they were not a deciding process, but merely approved what had already happened.

How were elections controlled?

Although all men over the age of 21 had the right to vote, the result was manipulated by making the system 'indirect'. It had three stages:

1. All voters in individual communes voted 10% of their number onto a Communal List.
2. Those on the Communal List voted 10% of their number onto a Departmental List.
3. Those on the Departmental List voted 10% of their number onto the National List.

At each stage the Prefect could put pressure on electors to return the government choice. In any case, getting on the National List did not mean obtaining office. The First Consul had the right to choose all officials and representatives from the list, thereby weeding out any opposition candidate who had managed to get through the three elections.

This system took too long to operate. It was replaced in 1802 when the communes were simply asked to elect a Board which would choose from the richest men in each Department.

Felix Markham, *Napoleon* (Weidenfeld & Nicolson, 1963) is a very readable account of the whole period, and his *Napoleon and the Awakening of Europe* (English University Press, 1958) is succinct and to the point. The most detailed treatment is to be found in Georges Lefebvre, *Napoleon* (Routledge & Kegan Paul, 1969), in two volumes.

THE KEY ISSUES

- How was the opposition eliminated?
- How did Napoleon enlist supporters?

THE KEY SKILLS

Investigation

Explanation

Copy the following spider diagram, then read carefully through this chapter and fill in the details under each heading. When you are drawing the diagram, remember to leave as much space as possible for your notes.

The Law

Police/Spies

Censorship

Jacobins/Workers

Emigrés

Awards and Titles

Propaganda

Coercion

Persuasion

How did Napoleon establish his hold on to power in France?

Government Centralisation

Disguising Dictatorship

Prefects

Appointments

Constitution

Plebiscites   Elections

Using your diagram, consider whether Napoleon ruled France through fear. Remember, you must show an ability to argue both for and against the statement, citing evidence in support of your assertions.

Napoleon as Emperor

THE LAW

Napoleon used the law to silence those who could not be persuaded. His power to appoint judges meant that the legal profession became reliant on him for salaries and advancement, thereby losing its independence. He set up 'special courts' outside the normal judicial system for political opponents. The favoured punishment for political offences was house arrest which restricted trouble-makers without making martyrs of them. But the regime could be harsh when necessary, and opponents were sometimes executed. Later in his reign, Napoleon overrode the entire legal process and claimed the right to imprison anyone for an indefinite period without trial. A centralised police system was set up under Joseph Fouché; its purpose was not only to monitor suspicious individuals, but also to gauge and report on the popular mood and so predict any threat to public order. In order to prevent Fouché from gaining too much power, the Paris police force was headed by L.-N. Dubois, part of whose job was to spy on Fouché. And, just to be sure, Napoleon employed his own informers to spy on everyone else!

Having seen the Paris disturbances of the early 1790s at first hand, Napoleon was especially concerned to control the urban workers. He attempted to ensure the supply of affordable bread through price controls and export restrictions on grain. However, he also reinforced the terms of the Chapelier Law banning trades unions; and he forced all workers to carry a *livret* (workbook) to monitor employment records and single out trouble-makers.

THE THREAT FROM ABROAD

Napoleon realised that he needed to defeat the Second Coalition quickly in order to gain a breathing space in which to consolidate his position at home. Once more he led an army across the Alps to defeat the Austrians. His victory at Marengo in June 1800, together with the (probably more significant) triumph of General Moreau at Hohenlinden in Germany a few months later, led to the Peace of Lunéville. In this treaty, Austria lost all influence in Italy and was left with little say in German affairs. Without a major European ally, Britain was willing to sign the Peace of Amiens in 1802.

THE THREAT AT HOME

Napoleon's position at home remained precarious despite Marengo. In his own mind the Jacobins posed a constant threat from the left. Meanwhile, on the right many royalists who thought the Coup de Brumaire might be a prelude to a Bourbon restoration were soon disappointed and began to plot themselves. On Christmas Eve 1800 royalist agents came close to assassinating Napoleon when they exploded a bomb as his coach passed on the way to the opera. Napoleon always believed that he could accommodate the royalists and that the Jacobins were his main threat. He therefore used the incident as an excuse to purge known Jacobins, over 100 of whom were sent into exile.

Despite continual plots, Napoleon tried to pacify the royalists with concessions. In 1800 he offered selected individuals the opportunity to return to the country. He followed this two years later with a general amnesty for all émigrés except those involved in the recent conspiracies. Although those who returned were to be kept under police observation for ten years, the terms appear generous. Many took the opportunity to rebuild their lives and, whilst some were willing to enter Napoleon's service, most preferred to stay clear of political involvement of any sort. The apparent weakness of the opposition gave Napoleon the opportunity to tighten his grip on power. In August 1802 a plebiscite confirmed him as First Consul for life.

There remained a hard core of royalists who were determined to oust him. In 1804 he had to act quickly to defeat yet another plot. It was thought that, as part of the plot, a Bourbon prince, the Duc d'Enghien, was to lead an émigré army into France. Napoleon had him kidnapped from a neighbouring German state and shot without any real evidence of his guilt. In 1803 the war against England had already resumed, but international shock at this unjustified act of brutality (together with the enticement of subsidies from the English) meant that in the autumn of 1805 France found herself at war with a Third Coalition which included both Austria and Russia.

THE EMPIRE AND ITS SERVANTS

In May 1804 Napoleon declared France an Empire with himself as Emperor. Pope Pius VI came to Paris to perform the coronation, but in a pre-arranged stunt Napoleon took the crown from his hands and crowned himself. The coronation was attended by a body of civil servants whom he had gathered from every social and political background in France. He offered careers to anyone based solely on their talent and their willingness to take orders. Once in his employ they were bound to him by generous gifts, enhanced social status and awards like the Legion of Honour, instituted in 1802 for exceptional service. He once said that 'men are led by baubles'. He demonstrated this in the use he made of rewards, titles and medals to maintain an individual's loyalty.

In 1808 he declared the beginning of a new 'imperial nobility'. Thousands of knights, barons and dukes were created, and many of them were given lavish grants of land and money to support their pretensions. It is noticeable that the vast majority of titles and awards were given to the army; the rest went to imperial civil servants. Very few manufacturers or merchants received awards.

Napoleon's attitude to the émigrés

'I am anxious that the Prefects should send you the lists of all amnestied persons and émigrés so that you may submit reports to me, one for each Department, and so that those who are recognised as being sensible, harmless and well disposed may receive permits from me, exempting them from supervision and restoring their civil rights. The art of government consists not only in punishing the wicked, but also in rewarding the good.'

From a letter of Napoleon to Fouché, 7 October 1804

Emigrés – nobles who fled abroad during the Revolution. They were often involved in conspiracies aimed at restoring the throne to the Bourbon claimant Louis XVIII (Louis XVI's brother).

Napoleon awards the first Legion of Honour

Napoleon's Domestic Reforms 1

In the period between his seizure of power and the resumption of the war in Europe, Napoleon introduced a number of important domestic reforms. His main aim was probably to end the disorder and discontent produced by the Revolution. He realised, however, that he had to be very careful not to upset those who had supported the Revolution.

THE PROBLEM WITH THE CATHOLIC CHURCH

The Catholic church suffered greatly during the Revolution. In 1789 its lands were confiscated and sold off. A year later, a government act known as the Civil Constitution of the Clergy provided for the election of priests and bishops by the laity, and ordered that all clergymen were to take an oath of loyalty to the Revolution. Some priests took the oath (becoming known as 'constitutional clergy'), but the majority ('refractory clergy') refused and became bitter opponents of the Revolution. Throughout the 1790s, refractory priests played a prominent role in stirring up anti-revolutionary rebellions within France, and royalist émigrés relied on the church to provide moral justification for their plots. This left many French people with an apparent choice between loyalty to God and loyalty to the government.

Napoleon had no particular religious views, but he did realise the importance of ending this damaging split in French society. He reasoned that if he could come to an agreement with the church, he could deprive the royalist cause of its greatest source of support. He also thought that the church might become a means of propaganda, encouraging loyalty to his regime throughout France. He had to be careful, however, for the bitterness was not one-sided: many old revolutionaries still hated the church and would oppose any concessions.

THE CONCORDAT

The negotiations, which began in June 1800, were assisted by two factors. First, a new pope, Pius VII, had recently been enthroned. He was much more moderate and flexible than his predecessor. Second, Napoleon's recent victory at Marengo left all Italy at his mercy. The negotiations therefore took place with the real threat of a French attack on Rome if they were unsuccessful.

The final agreement, which was reached in July 1801, appeared mutually beneficial. Certainly, the Roman Catholic church regained an official presence in France, then the world's largest Catholic state. But it was Napoleon who benefited most. Those who had bought

---

THE KEY ISSUES

- What did Napoleon hope to achieve through his Concordat with the Catholic church?
- Did the Concordat achieve his aim?

THE KEY SKILLS

Investigation
Interpretation
Explanation

Two views of the Concordat

Years later, when Napoleon was in exile on St Helena, Pius VII appealed to the British government for clemency:

'The pious and courageous initiative of 1801 moves us to forget and pardon the subsequent wrongs ... The Concordat was a Christian and heroic act of healing ...'

At the time Napoleon's motivation was not spiritual. He said:

'How can there be order in the state without religion? Society cannot exist without inequality of fortunes and inequality of fortunes cannot exist without religion. When a man is dying of hunger beside another who is stuffing himself, he cannot accept the difference if there is not an authority who tells him "God wishes it so."'

Geoffrey Ellis, *Napoleon* (Longman, 1997) gives a detailed and up-to-date treatment of the Concordat and the educational reforms. Equally valuable and easier to read is R. Ben Jones, *Napoleon: Man and Myth* (Hodder & Stoughton, 1977).

church land owed a debt of gratitude to him, for as part of the agreement the Pope confirmed their ownership. Many of the priests and bishops, who had so bitterly opposed the regime, now became its dependants. The state had the power to appoint them, and they had to take an oath of loyalty and conduct prayers for the Republic. Bereft of any hope of regaining confiscated church lands, up to 30 000 priests became reliant on government salaries. In return for surrendering to state power, the Catholic church did not even become the established religion with any special privileges over other denominations. It was not to be the religion of France, merely 'the religion of most Frenchmen'.

Despite the obvious power that Napoleon had gained over the church, he still feared the reaction when news of the agreement was received in France. So as to reduce any threat from anti-clerical revolutionaries, he simply added another section to the completed agreement without the Pope's consent. The additional 'Organic Articles' guaranteed equal rights for Protestants and gave the state even greater power over the church.

As Napoleon had intended, the damaging division between loyalty to the church and loyalty to the government was removed, and the loss of church support was a fatal blow to the émigré royalist cause. The success was not complete, however, for the restored priests never really became active supporters of the regime. They fulfilled their legal obligations, but did little more. In general the Concordat removed opponents, but did not create friends.

THE ECONOMY

Napoleon also realised that economic instability could threaten his hold on power. He was determined to avoid the violent fluctuations that had fuelled so many of the upheavals during the Revolution. His first target was to ensure a steady income for his government. Under the Directory, tax collection was the responsibility of local government. This meant a slow and uncertain supply of funds to Paris. Napoleon centralised tax raising, and although he retained private tax collectors (who took a share for their efforts), he made them deposit a proportion of the likely yield before collection. The reform was a great success. Tax returns were up to date within a year.

Napoleon's seizure of power was welcomed by the financial market, which hoped that a strong government would bring stability. He used this rising confidence to encourage several leading financiers to invest in a new Bank of France. At first, this was an independent institution handling tax collectors' deposits, state pensions and interest on government loans; but later it helped to control the money supply (and therefore its value) by assuming sole responsibility for the issue of paper currency. As confidence in the stability of the regime grew, the bank was able to reintroduce a large quantity of gold and silver coinage.

Napoleon's attempts to control the church are evident in his letters to the Minister for Church Affairs:

'12 May 1803. Please inform the Prefect of La Vendée and the Bishop of La Rochelle that I wish to give 150 francs to the 60 vicars who are best educated, and best behaved, and who show the greatest attachment to the Concordat, to religion, and to the government.'

'19 September 1805. Inform M. Robert, a priest at Bourges, of my displeasure at the extremely bad sermon he preached on 15 August.'

The way in which Napoleon used his power over the church is obvious from the Imperial Catechism, published in 1806:

'Christians owe ... the Emperor love, respect, obedience, fidelity, military service and taxes. "Why?"... because God ... has established him as our sovereign, and has given him the ministry of His power and image on earth.'

THE KEY ISSUES

- Was the Code Napoléon an enlightened document?
- Did Napoleon's reforms create 'equality' in France?

THE KEY SKILLS

Investigation
Interpretation
Empathy

Napoleon's supporters and opponents

Consider the following groups of people:

- High-ranking army officers
- Wealthy workshop owners
- Emigré nobles
- Refractory priests
- Peasants
- Urban workers
- Female intellectuals.

Explain how each group in the list might be affected by Napoleon's policies. You will have to refer to Chapters 2 and 3. Divide the list into three:

1. those who support him
2. those who appear indifferent
3. those who oppose him.

Does the group that opposes Napoleon coincide with those to whom he was most oppressive? Rank the groups in order, from the strongest supporters to the bitterest opponents. Can the whole class come to an agreed ranking?

Napoleon's Domestic Reforms 2

THE CODE NAPOLÉON

Before 1789 France had no fewer than 366 different local law codes, a situation further complicated by the existence of feudal customs, church regulations and royal proclamations. Although the Revolution swept away many of these laws, it failed to provide a single clear national code to replace them. Various revolutionary legal committees attempted to remedy this, but the task was an enormous one and, by 1800, although five drafts had been made, none was ever put into practice. The situation was made urgent by the vast amount of noble and church land which had been confiscated and sold off by the state. It was vital that the laws regulating and confirming ownership of property were made uniform and transparent.

In 1804 Napoleon introduced the Civil Code (renamed the Code Napoléon in 1807), completing the work of the revolutionary committees by providing France with a unified legal system. Other later codes went further by dealing with crime, commerce, the countryside and civil procedure.

The Code formalised the abolition of feudalism in all its legal forms. As such, it was an enlightened document. Its primary goal was to clarify property ownership, and in this respect it was an undoubted success. However, it was much more authoritarian than the first draft of 1794 would have been. It stressed the power of the father in the family, even to the point of allowing him temporarily to imprison disobedient children. The later codes showed an even harsher return to authoritarianism, with the introduction of branding for certain criminals and the loss of a hand for any child that killed its father.

It may have abolished feudalism, but it certainly did not guarantee equality. Women and urban workers were particularly discriminated against. In the early revolutionary drafts it seemed possible that women might achieve equal legal status with men, but the completed Civil Code reduced their rights to sign legal contracts and to inherit and dispose of property. Worse still were the laws affecting marital relationships. A husband's adultery was not viewed as grounds for a divorce unless he insisted that his mistress moved into the family home; but if a woman committed adultery her husband could have her gaoled for up to two years.

Napoleon held the urban lower class in contempt. His reign witnessed no social reform to improve the conditions of the poor. He did intervene to end abuse in some isolated cases, such as banning the employment of young children in mines; but there was no systematic attempt to end abuse and injustice. He was much more concerned with controlling workers through repressive measures than through concessions, and although the Code denied the right of either workers or employers combining against each other, the punishments for workers were much greater than those for employers.

Napoleon claimed that he took more pride in the Code than he did in all his military victories, but it was largely the work of the legal experts of the Council of State. Although Napoleon attended almost half its sessions, it was a document that relied on specialist expertise which Napoleon did not possess. It is likely that Napoleon made two real contributions to the Code: first, his own authoritarianism probably inspired some of its less enlightened provisions; second, his impatient, forceful character meant that, unlike all the others, this Code got beyond the draft stage and into practical application.

EDUCATION

Napoleon was suspicious of the existing church schools and the progressive ideas of some of the existing independent schools. In 1802 he declared the foundation of a new type of state school called the *lycée*, which would teach a narrow curriculum and train students to serve the state in adult life. Almost one third of the places in the *lycée* were reserved for army officers, but they were never really popular with other parents who were put off by the high fees, military-style discipline and harsh punishments (for students and teachers!).

Instead, the church schools flourished throughout the Napoleonic period, and, partly to ensure a degree of control over them, Napoleon set up the Imperial University to oversee the curriculum and to carry out inspections.

Predictably, no effort was made to provide education for girls or for the poor. He said that women should 'stick to knitting' and he believed that workers should be taught no more than was necessary to carry out menial tasks. The absence of a system of primary education and the fees charged by the secondary schools meant that Napoleon's ideal of 'careers open to talent' never extended below the bourgeoisie.

Napoleon and the Revolution

The relationship between Napoleon's domestic policies and the ideals of the Revolution is a very complex issue and often appears in A-level exam papers. Consider these four major revolutionary ideals:

- **Liberty** – by which most revolutionaries meant liberty of expression and legal rights;
- **Equality** – by which they meant 'careers open to talent', i.e. equal opportunities based solely on ability;
- **Fraternity** – by which they meant that the government should show a humane interest in the welfare of its citizens;
- **Representative government** – which meant that the government should be chosen by its citizens and should represent their opinions.

Copy the diagram below. Then read carefully through Chapters 2 and 3, making notes in the relevant boxes. Each ideal has 'Yes/No' areas that will enable you to put forward a balanced argument to answer the following question: *Did Napoleon betray the ideals of the Revolution?*

Liberty		Equality	
Yes	No	Yes	No
	Did Napoleon Betray the Revolution?		
Yes	No	Yes	No
Representative Government		**Fraternity**	

THE KEY ISSUE

● How did Napoleon defeat the Third Coalition?

THE KEY SKILLS

Chronology
Assessment
Explanation

'Little Johnny Bull' defies Napoleon's attempts at world domination: a British cartoon of October 1806

The terms of the Treaty of Pressburg, December 1805

Loss of Venetia, the last Austrian possession in Italy, ceded to the Kingdom of Italy. Dalmatia becomes a part of the French Empire. Napoleon's allies Bavaria and Württemberg gain land at Austria's expense and are made independent kingdoms. Austrian influence in Germany is effectively ended.

Napoleon's Victories in Europe

THE THIRD COALITION

The Peace of Amiens was viewed by both England and France as nothing more than a temporary truce. Commercial and colonial rivalries soon led to a renewal of war between the two countries in 1803. Napoleon began to assemble a new Army of England, making plans for a cross-channel invasion from a central base at Boulogne.

The British prime minister, William Pitt, tried to avert the threat of invasion by offering continental allies large subsidies if they were willing to challenge Napoleon. The European monarchs, already outraged at the murder of the Duc d'Enghien (see page 21) and Napoleon's expansionist policies in southern Germany, found that British gold was the final incentive they needed to go to war. By the autumn of 1805, Britain had been joined by Austria, Russia and Sweden in a Third Coalition. Of the important European powers, only Prussia remained uncommitted – bribed into neutrality by Napoleon's promise of Hanover (then ruled by the King of England).

THE DEFEAT OF AUSTRIA

With a combined strength of around half a million men, the coalition partners had some cause for confidence. One Austrian army, under General Mack, was forming in southern Germany to threaten Napoleon's ally Bavaria, while another waited in Bohemia for the arrival of a large Russian army under General Kutusov and Tsar Alexander I. Napoleon realised the danger of allowing these forces to unite and, in August 1805, he broke camp at Boulogne, moving his (renamed) Grand Army into Germany in the hope of defeating his enemies separately. The Grand Army moved with great speed in a web of separate corps, stretching over a front of more than 100 miles (160 km). Mack was caught and surrounded at Ulm in Germany. He was forced to surrender an army of 49 000 men with barely a struggle.

The second Austrian army, realising the danger of their own isolated position, quickly retreated east to join their Russian allies. While in pursuit, Napoleon heard news of the destruction of the French fleet at Trafalgar by a British force under Nelson. He realised that an invasion of Britain was no longer possible, but he was determined to leave Pitt without allies in Europe. On 2 December 1805 he crushed the combined Austro-Russian army at Austerlitz. The Russians withdrew into their own territory, leaving Austria to surrender and be subjected to the harsh terms of the Treaty of Pressburg.

THE HUMILIATION OF PRUSSIA

Napoleon's dominant position in Central Europe was now an obvious threat to Prussian independence. At this time Prussia was still considered a major military power. A generation before, its army had been led to stunning victories over its neighbours by King Frederick the Great. Many observers believed, therefore, that the ensuing contest would be a close-fought and lengthy affair. Unfortunately, although large and well-trained, the Prussian army was led by ageing commanders whose idea of warfare had not changed since the previous century. Pitted against a veteran army schooled in the latest tactics, the Prussians didn't stand a chance.

In September 1806 Prussia made the terrible mistake of entering a war against France without the support of any effective allies. Instead of holding back and attempting to join up with the Russians, King Frederick William immediately sent two armies south to challenge the French in Germany. Placing himself between the two armies, Napoleon sent Marshal Davout to hold one Prussian force at Auerstadt, while he confronted the other at Jena. Two separate battles took place on the same day. Both resulted in comprehensive French victories.

THE TREATY OF TILSIT

Frederick William led the remnants of his army east to join with the Russians who continued to defy the French. It was vital for Napoleon to conclude this part of the war before Austria re-entered hostilities on his southern flank. Throughout the winter of 1806–1807, he tried in vain to force a decisive engagement. In desperately cold weather at Eylau in February 1807, he fought a bloody draw. It was not until June, when he caught the Tsar's army at Friedland, that Napoleon was able to inflict a decisive enough defeat to make the Russians sue for peace.

Tsar Alexander met Napoleon on a raft moored between their two armies at Tilsit on the River Niemen. The impressionable Alexander was soon captivated by Napoleon's charisma. The two became allies, agreeing to divide Europe between them into spheres of influence. Napoleon was to have a free hand in Central Europe, while Alexander was to receive French support in extending Russian influence in both the Baltic and the Balkans. Russia's former allies suffered most from this agreement. Prussia was forced to accept humiliating terms, and Alexander promised to mediate with Britain in order to create a general peace. If Britain refused his peace offer, then Russia would declare war. In the meantime, Russia joined Denmark, Sweden and Prussia in closing their ports to British goods

---

Napoleon's view of Prussia

'The idea that Prussia could take me on single-handed is too absurd to merit discussion ... Her cabinet is so contemptible, her king so weak, and her court so dominated by young officers in search of adventure, that no one can depend upon her. She will go on acting as she has acted – arming today, disarming tomorrow; standing by, sword in hand, while the battle is fought, and then making terms with the conqueror.'

Letter of Napoleon to Talleyrand, 12 September 1806

How the Treaty of Tilsit affected Prussia

Loss of one third of her territory, largely land settled by Poles, and formed into the Grand Duchy of Warsaw. Payment of a large indemnity (French troops to occupy the country until it was paid). Her army is restricted to 42 000 men.

If you can remember the name, year and opponent fought for each battle mentioned in this chapter, it will serve as a useful *aide-mémoire* for the entire period, as well as being of value in exam essays. There are seven battles in total – close the book and see if you can remember them.

THE KEY ISSUES

- What were Napoleon's strengths?
- What were the allies' weaknesses?
- Why did the Third Coalition find it impossible to coordinate their diplomatic and military effort?

THE KEY SKILLS

Investigation
Interpretation
Explanation

Charles Esdaile, *The Wars of Napoleon* (Longman, 1995) is a thorough treatment of every aspect, from the tactical to the strategic. David Chandler, *Napoleon* (Weidenfeld & Nicolson, 1973), Chapter 6 covers many of the issues dealt with in this chapter.

Europe in 1805

Consult a map of Europe before Napoleon's victories. You will notice three key differences from the Europe of today:

1. Germany was divided into 360 states. Austria had most influence in the area, but Prussia was also a significant power.
2. Italy was divided into a number of states. Again Austria had some influence in the north, but this was under challenge from the French who had already annexed the state of Piedmont in the north-east.
3. There was no state of Poland. This had been partitioned by Austria, Russia and Prussia in the early 1790s. Polish patriots continued to hope for their independence.

The Reasons for Napoleon's Success

DIVISION AND UNITY

Napoleon's enemies were hopelessly divided and tended to pursue their own self-interest at the expense of the common good. This division meant that up to 1813 Napoleon never had to face the united military capacity of his enemies.

All three of the great eastern powers were willing to abandon their allies when the need arose. In 1805 Napoleon was able to buy Prussian neutrality by offering Hanover. This delayed Prussian entry into the war until Austria had been defeated and Russia was too severely weakened to offer immediate assistance. During the campaign of 1807, Austria assembled an army of 120 000 men (known as the Army of Neutrality, for obvious reasons) and could have threatened Napoleon's southern flank at a crucial time; but the opportunity was missed through timidity in the wake of the Battle of Austerlitz, and Russia was left to face the Grand Army alone. After his defeat at Friedland, a despairing Tsar Alexander was willing to jettison his former allies and act out of individual self-interest – to the point of offering to make war on Britain on Napoleon's behalf.

Napoleon's situation reveals a startling contrast to the divisions within the Third Coalition. He commanded a single national army which did not have to coordinate its movements with distant allies. All the necessary organisation could be carried out in his own head. And, unlike the allies, he had a single war aim which he pursued through his sole command of diplomacy and without reference to any other interest but his own.

COORDINATION

From the beginning of the 1805 campaign, the allies misjudged Napoleon's intentions. Austria may have believed that the main theatre of operations would once again be northern Italy. But by sending their best commander, Archduke Charles, and many of their best troops to this area, they had no influence on subsequent events. And, when Napoleon unexpectedly chose to enter Germany, he found the allies unprepared, with Mack's Austrian army too far west to get support from the advancing Russians. In 1806 Prussia and Russia repeated the mistake. The disaster at Jena occurred because Prussia foolishly advanced against Napoleon without waiting for Russian help. Poor coordination was not the only allied weakness. They were also dogged by sheer incompetence. This was compounded by the fact that all three respective monarchs accompanied their armies and interfered in decision-making, thereby ensuring defeat.

Whereas the allies bickered between themselves, Napoleon pursued a single goal, the defeat of the allied army. He did not suffer from the debilitating split between military and political objectives which led the allies to disaster, because he combined the role of commander-in-chief with that of head of state. This enabled him to put the resources of the state at the direct and immediate use of the military. Unlike the allied generals, he could meet all his necessary military needs through a simple decree which would have immediate effect.

ARMIES, COMMANDERS AND BUREAUCRACIES

Allied armies were for the most part commanded by ageing generals whose ideas had been formulated in the previous century and who had failed to learn from the changes that had taken place in warfare during the 1790s. These armies moved with slow predictability, and on the battlefield they used formal linear tactics with insufficient light infantry. Napoleon's Grand Army, by contrast, was hardened and confident, and had developed and perfected its methods from recent experience. The superiority of the French army has led historians to question the significance of Napoleon's personal contribution to the victories of 1805–1807, but the very least that can be said is that he was far superior to his opposing commanders and that this had an influence on the triumph of the French. (A fuller treatment of the military aspects of the wars of Napoleon can be found in Chapter 5.)

Napoleon could not hope to match the potential human and material resources of his combined enemies. However, they were incapable of pressing home this advantage, because the inferiority of their administrative systems made it impossible for them to realise their full potential. The bureaucratic reforms that took place during the Revolution made France the most efficient state in Europe. It meant that French resources were more readily accessible when required. By contrast, the allies relied on antiquated systems of conscription and taxation which failed to marshal the necessary resources needed to counter Napoleon. If he were to be effectively challenged, the old monarchies would need to coordinate their efforts, reform their tactics and strategy, and resource ever larger armies.

Napoleon's conquest of Europe

Draw up two lists, one of Napoleon's advantages and the other of the allies' disadvantages. Each list must deal with resources, coordination, tactics, command and competence. Where possible each factor included on your list must be supported by an example or an explanation.

Use your two lists to answer the following question: *Is Napoleon's conquest of Europe largely explained by the weakness of his enemies?* Remember, good marks in History essays usually go to the student who shows the ability to understand and support both sides of any debate before reaching a personal conclusion.

Command problems of the allies

'The [allied] plans were riddled with false assumptions and shoddy staff work. Napoleon's intention was wholly miscalculated. The Austrians were courting a great risk by moving into Germany and Italy before their allies appeared. Moreover the Austrian staff, incredible as it may seem, failed to take into account the ten days difference between the German and Russian calendars – and their expectation that the Russians would appear by 20 October was to prove a fatal miscalculation.'

David Chandler, *Napoleon*, 1973

'Mack [was] secretly authorised to ignore [Archduke] Charles, still further confusion was caused by the fact that [Emperor] Francis began to interfere in operations ... theoretically [the Russians were] commanded by Kutusov, the preponderant influence was actually wielded by the Tsar, who thought himself a great military commander. The Prussians had a proper commander-in-chief ... but he was old and weak ... his orders were flouted, sabotaged or simply disregarded.'

Charles Esdaile, *The Wars of Napoleon*, 1995

THE KEY ISSUES

- How did warfare change as a result of the Revolution?
- What debt did Napoleon owe to existing military developments for his success?

THE KEY SKILLS

Investigation
Analysis
Explanation

Strategy – the plans devised by generals on maps

Tactics – the methods used by troops on the battlefield

Division – a force of around 10 000 men usually consisting of cavalry, infantry and artillery

Skirmishers – troops who moved and fired independently. Unlike ordinary infantry, they did not fight shoulder to shoulder, but stayed around 10 feet (3 m) apart. Often called light infantry.

Column – a formation around 16 men deep used for charging into hand-to-hand combat with the enemy

Line – a formation, either two or three men deep, for firing on the enemy

Brigade – a force of 2000 to 5000 men, usually consisting of either infantry or cavalry alone

Corps – a force of around 30 000 men

Battalion – a tactical infantry unit of around 800 men

The Changing Face of Warfare

WARFARE IN THE 18TH CENTURY

The wars of the 18th century were limited in both their scale and their aims. War was viewed as an activity pursued by princes for their own narrow dynastic objectives. As such, war did not directly involve most of civil society – their sole responsibility was to pay the limited taxes necessary for the upkeep of the military. The rank-and-file of every army was held in contempt by respectable society and was made up of foreign mercenaries, social misfits and conscripted peasants who were all subjected to ferocious punishments to ensure discipline. Soldiers like these often had little individual enthusiasm for battle, so they were drilled to move with unthinking efficiency and to fire in group volleys.

Even the very poor viewed soldiering with disdain. With most armies, recruits were hard to find and easy to lose through desertion, sickness and battle. Generals, therefore, often preferred to conserve manpower by avoiding battles and trying to win campaigns by manoeuvring to place the enemy at a disadvantage. Campaign movement became slow and predictable because of the need to keep in touch with supplies, which were carried in slow-moving wagon trains or held in static magazines. Furthermore, the threat of desertion meant that commanders dared not risk night marches or movement through rough terrain. Lack of surprise or initiative meant that, when battles did take place, both sides employed the same linear tactics, with long lines of men and scattered artillery firing at each other from close range. The result was too often a very bloody stalemate.

THE REVOLUTION IN WARFARE

The French Revolution completely transformed warfare. The war that broke out in 1791 differed dramatically from the conflicts of the preceding century. Instead of being a limited dynastic squabble which would end in the transfer of a few provinces at the negotiating table, this was an ideological war in which political opposites fought for their very survival. In order to save France from the invader, the Jacobin government assumed enormous new powers over the citizen during the winter of 1793–1794. These included conscription, a measure that changed the French army and the way it fought.

The new army was shorn of many of its older aristocratic officers and professional mercenary troops. They were replaced by an officer corps of talented and dynamic young men who were willing to experiment with new ideas, and a rank-and-file of enthusiastic and well-motivated patriots. These were men of a completely different stamp to the old army personnel. The new soldiers were often eager to fight and showed a high level of personal initiative, but they lacked discipline. This made the introduction of new tactics essential, if France was to survive the onslaught of the European monarchies.

NEW STRATEGY AND TACTICS

On campaign, French commanders actively sought battle in the hope of wearing the enemy down and making their superior numbers decisive. As armies grew in size, they became more cumbersome to manoeuvre on the existing road system, so the French armies were split up into divisions and moved along several different roads at once. It was impossible for the chaotic revolutionary governments to keep such huge numbers supplied, so they took to living off the land. This also made their movements faster and much more difficult for the enemy to predict.

On the battlefield, a more fluid system of warfare appeared which took advantage of the new troops' initiative. It also required less training and discipline. Soldiers were allowed to act as skirmishers, moving and firing individually, and the infantry column was often preferred to the line. The idea of the column was to rely less on an exchange of fire (which required lengthy training to be effective) and more on the use of the bayonet charge. This would either intimidate opponents into disorganised withdrawal or smash their line through weight of numbers.

NAPOLEON AND THE NEW WARFARE

Napoleon was not an original military thinker. He added nothing new to the type of warfare developed during the Revolution. Like many of his contemporaries, his theories of warfare were heavily influenced by 18th-century military writers and by his own experience. The major difference between the wars of the Revolution and the wars of Napoleon was the scale on which they were fought. Instead of using the brigade to manoeuvre, Napoleon used the corps; in place of the artillery battery of perhaps eight guns, he devised the grand battery of over 100; and later he would use the divisional infantry column instead of the battalion.

A typical revolutionary battle. The diagram below will give you some idea of how the new tactics worked in an ideal situation.

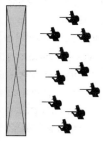

Stage 1.
French skirmishers fire at the allied army as it slowly draws itself into line, demoralising the troops and making deployment difficult.

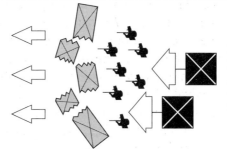

Stage 3.
Preceded by skirmishers, the infantry attacks the shaken enemy line in column, forcing it to retreat.

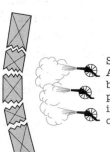

Stage 2.
A concentrated battery of artillery pieces blows a hole in the weakest part of the enemy line.

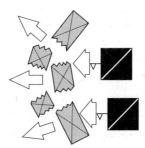

Stage 4.
French cavalry now pours into the gap created by the infantry and artillery. They pursue the defeated enemy and prevent it from making an orderly withdrawal.

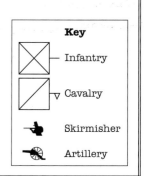

Key

⊠	Infantry
⧄	Cavalry
—	Skirmisher
—	Artillery

THE KEY ISSUES

- Did Napoleon's ability decline in later years?
- How did his enemies learn from their defeats?

THE KEY SKILLS

Investigation

Analysis

Napoleon as a military commander

The diagram below compares Napoleon's personal role in his victory and defeat with the part played by other circumstances beyond his control. Read this chapter carefully and collect the evidence for each case in the relevant boxes.

Why were the French victorious?

Napoleon	Other

Why were the French defeated?

Napoleon	Other

Use your diagram to answer the following question: *Was Napoleon a military genius?* Remember, in order to answer this question properly you must not only debate his successes and failures, but also ask whether victory and defeat were down to Napoleon personally or whether they were the result of broader circumstances not of his making.

Napoleon as a Commander

NAPOLEON'S ART OF WAR

Napoleon believed that the aim of each campaign was to bring the enemy army to battle on favourable terms and destroy its ability to resist. Modern historians have compared his strategy to 20th-century *blitzkrieg*, because he envisaged short violent campaigns placing as little strain as possible on his supply and communications.

Central to his planning for any campaign was the corps system. This involved splitting his force up into a number of mini-armies moving along roughly parallel routes within a day's march of each other. Apart from quickening the movement of his army and easing supply problems, this gave Napoleon a significant strategic advantage. With so many troops advancing over such a broad front, it was very difficult for an enemy commander to guess his intentions. Each corps was composed of enough troops to be able to hold its own against a superior enemy until it was reinforced by other corps, which would 'march to the sound of the guns' when one of their number was attacked. If the enemy chose to attack an apparently isolated corps, he would soon find French reinforcements arriving quickly, often on his flank or from the rear. If he chose to stay put, he would be surrounded by the separate corps like the tentacles of an octopus.

THE GENIUS OF NAPOLEON

Such is the power of Napoleon's legend that historians have only recently begun to question his ability as a commander. Those who denigrate his ability point to his extraordinary good luck, the incompetence of his opposition, his lack of originality and the relative excellence of the Grand Army before 1808. His broader strategic errors are more obvious. He seriously underestimated the ability of the Spanish people to resist his will, and it is an inescapable fact that the enormous losses incurred in the Russian campaign were down to his own poor judgement (see Chapter 7).

On the positive side, there is no doubt that he had the ability to plan in a grand manner and manoeuvre hundreds of thousands of troops with amazing precision. Nor can his flexibility be doubted, for, though he always made detailed plans, he was also a superb opportunist, able to depart from any plan to gain significant advantage. He inherited a fine military machine, but his incredible ability to inspire its individual soldiers made it even more formidable. He was a master of propaganda and self-advertisement, but he also fostered genuine loyalty among the French soldiers. Long after the decline of nationalism, which had inspired the army to defend the frontiers of France, Napoleon encouraged greater effort with appeals to 'la gloire'.

THE ENEMY IMPROVE

After their catastrophic defeats of 1805–1807, Napoleon's enemies worked hard to match the quality of his Grand Army. They belatedly adopted many of the tactics developed by the French during the revolutionary wars. States like Russia, Prussia and Austria recruited increasing numbers of light infantry, simplified their drill, practised the use of the infantry column and developed their own corps systems. Although they shrank from universal conscription to the regular army, Austria and Prussia increased the numbers available to their commanders by recruiting militia units for second line duties.

The secret of French success was the creation of a national army of self-motivated troops. It has similarly been argued that Napoleon's military decline lay in nationalist reactions to French oppression. In Russia and Spain, irregular forces more or less spontaneously sprang up to oppose the French in a new kind of guerrilla warfare. In Prussia, the humiliation of 1806 led to the triumph of a group of military reformers motivated more by the notion of a wider German identity than their loyalty to the King of Prussia.

NAPOLEON DECLINES

Napoleon's ability as a military commander appeared to decline after 1808. Growing fat, he suffered a range of medical complaints which sapped his enormous energy, making campaigning difficult. His strategic judgement failed him on a number of occasions and he seems to have lost much of his tactical subtlety. At Aspern-Essling, Borodino and Waterloo, he simply sent massed ranks forward in a bid to crush the enemy through sheer weight of numbers. In all three cases, the result was appalling casualties and either stalemate or defeat.

The interpretation that puts such a premium on Napoleon's alleged loss of ability may be too simple. For one thing, if he was declining as a commander, there was no evidence of it in his final campaign of 1814. Although heavily outnumbered, he showed all his old energy when defending Paris against several allied armies. For another, it could be argued that the decisive factor was not Napoleon, but the size and quality of his army. The Grand Army that conquered Europe in the two years after 1805 was a professional French force with a high proportion of veterans. The losses incurred in these campaigns and in Spain after 1808 meant that by 1812 many of Napoleon's soldiers were raw and reluctant foreign conscripts lacking both experience and training. Small wonder, then, that he abandoned subtle manoeuvres. Perhaps he had come to feel that his troops were only capable of blunt frontal attacks. Throughout the period the size of armies increased steadily, and it is possible that this was an important factor in Napoleon's crude tactics. He operated without the aid of either a trained general staff or modern communications technology, and his armies simply became too big for him to control.

Napoleon's strategies

Three of Napoleon's favourite strategies, as identified by historian David Chandler:

1. Over-stretching the enemy by making them respond to a number of feint attacks before delivering an all-out thrust at their weakest point. Used at the start of the Russian campaign of 1812.
2. The Central Position. When faced with more than one opponent, get between them and hold the one off with a small force, while crushing the other. Used at the Battles of Jena and Auerstadt against Prussia in 1806.
3. Envelopment. Tempt the enemy to attack an apparently weak and isolated corps so as surround him when he advances. Used at Ulm in 1805 against the Austrian General Mack.

You can make a good start with Hew Strachan, *European Armies and the Conduct of War* (George Allen & Unwin, 1983), or Michael Howard, *War in European History* (Oxford University Press, 1976). Owen Connelly, *Blundering to Glory* (Wilmington, Del., 1988) and Corelli Barnett, *Bonaparte* (Allen & Unwin, 1978) question Napoleon's ability as a commander. David Chandler, *Campaigns of Napoleon* (Weidenfeld & Nicolson, 1966) is a very detailed (and long) work. You could also read Chapter 6 of his *Napoleon* (Weidenfeld & Nicolson, 1973).

THE KEY ISSUES

- What was Napoleon's intention in creating the Empire?
- How were the people of Europe affected by Napoleon's rule?

THE KEY SKILLS

Investigation
Interpretation
Explanation

Junta – a Spanish revolutionary committee
French Empire – for the purposes of this chapter, this will mean all those lands heavily influenced by France

Napoleon and Europe 1

Map of Napoleon's Empire, 1812

Allied States Denmark, Sweden, Austria and Prussia were classed as French allies and were compelled to pay occasional subsidies and provide troops for military expeditions. Prussia and Austria, for example, were forced to provide contingents to flank the Grand Army which invaded Russia in 1812.

France Expanded to include Belgium (1795), Piedmont (1802), the Papal States (1809), Holland and the north German coast (1810) and Catalonia (1812). By 1812 one third of French Departments were non-French speaking. The new Departments were subject to all the reforms that applied to France.

Spain Never really became a settled part of the Empire. Joseph Bonaparte was made king (1808), but he had to share power with the various juntas and the French commanders who were in control of 'military districts' – with authority to ignore him where they felt it necessary. The French were supported by a small group of middle-class Spaniards. Although reform of the church and the abolition of feudalism were announced, this had no practical effect in the country at large.

Confederation of the Rhine Napoleon redrew the map of Germany in 1806. The number of states was reduced, creating a series of client states which were big enough to ease effective exploitation, but not strong enough to take an independent line from France. Usually the old rulers kept their thrones and expanded their territory by absorbing the very small states. In these states, reform was left to the individual monarch. The new state of Westphalia was later added and ruled by Jérôme Bonaparte who introduced the full range of French reforms.

Grand Duchy of Warsaw Created (1807) from Prussian-Polish territory and later expanded (1809) with Austrian-Polish lands. Theoretically ruled by the King of Saxony, but effectively a French protectorate. Feudalism abolished, but nobility remained dominant.

Kingdom of Naples Ruled by Joseph Bonaparte (1806–1808), then Marshal Murat (Napoleon's brother-in-law). Financial and tax reforms were attempted, feudalism was abolished and some church property was taken by the state. But, because of local opposition, neither the Code Napoléon nor the Concordat were introduced.

Kingdom of Italy Napoleon made himself King of Italy until 1811 when his infant son became 'King of Rome'. The area was governed by Napoleon's stepson Eugène Beauharnais as vice-regent. Eugène was the most loyal of the family rulers and followed Napoleon's instructions to the letter. The full range of French legal, financial, military and religious reforms were introduced.

The Bonaparte dynasty – top line (l. to r.): Josephine Beauharnais, Napoleon Bonaparte, Marie Louise; second line (l. to r.): Joseph Bonaparte, Louis Bonaparte, Eugène Bonaparte, Lucien Bonaparte; third line (l. to r.): Jérôme Bonaparte, Napoleon II (King of Rome); the rest are female members of the dynasty

The French Empire officially consisted only of those territories contained within the expanded borders of France, but Napoleon's influence extended well beyond France to a number of theoretically independent allies and satellite states ruled by members of his family. What were Napoleon's intentions for the future of these two states?

A UNIFIED EUROPE?

From 1810 onwards, Napoleon began to absorb neighbouring satellite and allied states directly into France. This has led some historians to cast him as the 'first great European', a man with the clear long-term goal of creating a single European superstate ruled directly from Paris. In reality this expansion was probably more to do with his need to enforce the Continental System, gain more direct access to neighbouring resources and end the defiance of relatives who ruled satellite states.

The birth of a son to Marie Louise (see page 39) meant that Napoleon was no longer reliant on his relatives to continue the family line. This was convenient, for he was quickly becoming disillusioned with the ingratitude and disloyalty of his brothers and had probably already decided to act against them. In 1810 Louis was removed from the Dutch throne and Holland was annexed by France; Jérôme conceded a portion of Westphalia to France and plans were laid to remove him altogether; Joseph lost what little power he had over Spanish affairs; and Murat's poor relations with the Emperor meant that he only narrowly held on to the Neapolitan throne.

Ultimately, Napoleon's policies may have led to a European superstate, but this would have been created solely for the convenience and security of France and the efficiency of the Empire. Napoleon therefore does not deserve the title 'the first great European'.

A EUROPE OF NATION STATES?

After his downfall, Napoleon tried to justify his Empire by claiming that he sought to promote nation states in Germany, Italy and Poland. Although he did rationalise state boundaries within Germany and Italy, he was no respecter of nationality and blatantly ignored the wishes of those he ruled. He established a Polish state in the form of the Duchy of Warsaw, but the Poles never gained independence. Instead, veiled promises of future statehood were cynically used to encourage a massive military effort from the Polish people.

Napoleon's redrawn map of Europe did not include any free nation states ruled by native governments. Instead, he favoured conveniently sized units governed by foreign prefects or monarchs of his choice. The ideal state unit was large enough to be of military and economic value, but too small to maintain an independent line from France.

The performance of the Bonaparte dynasty

Napoleon had intended to exert complete control over the dynasty and use its members as organs of his own power, but they had different ideas:

'They showed naive and comic vanity, living in exaggerated luxury, surrounding themselves with favourites, creating court duties and marshals, and instituting decorations. Furthermore, they shared their mother's uncertainty about Napoleon's future, and attributed his success to chance. They did not intend to be dragged down in his fall and so tried to make themselves popular [with their subjects].'

G. Lefebvre, Napoleon, 1969

In Naples, Murat attempted to avoid adherence to the Continental System and tried to win popularity by championing Neopolitan interests against those of France. In Westphalia, Jérôme was famous for his extravagance. In Holland, Louis refused to close his ports to British goods or introduce conscription.

Napoleon's view of the rights of peoples

'I think it ridiculous for you to tell me that the people of Westphalia do not agree ... If you listen to what the people think, you won't do anything at all. If the people refuse what makes for their own welfare, they are guilty of anarchy, and the first duty of the prince is to punish them.'

From a letter of Napoleon to Jérôme, 1810

THE KEY ISSUE

● How and why did the people of Europe resist Napoleon's rule?

THE KEY SKILL

Investigation

Charles Esdaile, *The Wars of Napoleon* (Longman, 1995) and Geoffrey Ellis, *The Napoleonic Empire* (Macmillan, 1991), have argued that Napoleon saw the Empire simply as a short-term source of plunder.

Why did Napoleon create the Empire?

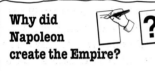

Draw the diagram below and use this chapter to fill in the details under each heading.

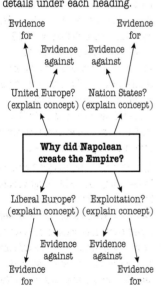

Using your diagram, answer the following question: *'Napoleon's Empire was created solely for the resources that it provided.' Do you agree?* Remember, you must examine the other alternatives before coming to a conclusion.

Napoleon and Europe 2

A LIBERAL EUROPE?

For over a century, historians accepted the idea that Napoleon's Empire swept away aristocratic and church privilege, ushering in a modern era with careers open to talent, religious toleration and constitutional government based on elected institutions. More recently, this picture has been revised to show the limits of Napoleon's impact on Europe.

Imperial reform was not an even process. Its extent depended on the status of the territory (a satellite or ally), the length of time it had been under French rule and the strength of local resistance. To many of the allied states within the Confederation of the Rhine, reform was a matter of choice for the ruler. Thus, while the kings of Württemberg and Bavaria accepted the need for greater efficiency to meet the Empire's demands for men and money, the King of Saxony introduced no reform at all. Even in the family-run satellites, reform was often uneven. The Code Napoléon was never introduced in Naples; in Poland, Jews were not granted religious equality; and in Spain, the Concordat was heavily modified in an attempt to avoid offending Catholic feeling.

Napoleon did not introduce reforms in order to liberate Europe, but in order to win support. Where reforms were likely to be unpopular, they were modified, and where they might actually arouse opposition, they were sometimes not implemented at all. In many areas, the reforms were intended to destroy the power of existing interest groups such as the church, the nobility or the guilds, and replace them with the more compliant urban middle class.

Napoleon was usually careful to avoid alienating the nobility in case they might eventually be won round. Therefore, although feudalism was abolished, the nobility held on to much of their land and wealth, especially in areas like Poland where few middle-class collaborators could be found. The position of the middle class may have improved, but the peasants and workers never felt the benefit. The abolition of feudalism did not mean a social revolution. In many territories, the peasantry was put in a worse position because the nobility now held the land without any of the traditional obligations to their tenants. Similarly, tax reforms in the satellite regimes ensured that the tax burden fell disproportionately on the poor. The failure to spread the benefits of Empire beyond a small élite of collaborators meant that support outside France was never deep-rooted.

Although many of the Empire's satellites and allies issued constitutions and set up assemblies, this did not herald a liberal political revolution. As in France, the impressive array of assemblies was really only camouflage for dictatorship. In Spain and Naples, the assembly existed only on paper. In the Kingdom of Italy, it was quickly closed down after the first sign of opposition. Constitutions in the other territories followed the French model, with a powerful executive and a powerless assembly chosen from a narrow élite section of society, without regard to the majority of the population. Imperial assemblies were not meant to be representative, but purely a means of rewarding influential local collaborators.

AN EXPLOITED EUROPE

Reforms were attempted in most areas of the Empire, but these were often aimed at increasing the effectiveness of government in policing, taxation, currency and customs. They were not concerned with meeting any popular demand. To Napoleon, the main idea of reform was to replace the chaotic administration of the old regime with a more efficient series of agencies allowing for maximum exploitation of each territory's resources. This exploitation was intended to secure his own position in France by transferring the costs of war on to his allies and his defeated enemies.

Napoleon had every intention of making sure that France was the main beneficiary of the exclusion of British goods from Europe. Each satellite was compelled to negotiate trade treaties which were highly favourable to France. Some of them were made to sell their raw materials to France and purchase finished goods in return; while others had to accept tariffs on their exports to France, but were not allowed to counter with their own taxes on French goods. Napoleon even outlawed mechanisation in some parts of Europe in the hope of stimulating French industrialisation.

Where money was required in a hurry, Napoleon issued cash demands to his allies and made defeated enemy states pay huge indemnities. In order to reduce the burden of conscription on France, all the allied states were required to provide a large contingent for the Grand Army. By 1812, even modest-sized states were having to maintain improbably large military establishments, as Napoleon forced his allies almost to double the size of their armies prior to the invasion of Russia. He offered no assistance with the cost of this massive military build-up. His sole aim was to reduce the burden on France. He deliberately stationed over 1 million French troops outside France to make the allied states responsible for the enormous cost of their upkeep.

In order to ensure their loyalty, Napoleon gave his marshals vast tracts of land outside France. This meant a serious loss of income to the already burdened states. And the situation was made much worse by the effects of the Continental System, which destroyed trade in many parts of Europe. The result of this limitless exploitation was drastic tax rises (the tax burden did not increase in France until 1813) and state bankruptcy for faithful allies such as Westphalia, the Kingdom of Italy and the Duchy of Warsaw.

Popular resistance to the French

There were surprisingly few popular rebellions against French rule. Apart from Spain, armed risings only took place in Calabria (1806) and the Tyrol (1809). Most resistance was passive, taking the form of draft evasion and desertion from the allied contingents, refusal to pay tax and failure to comply with laws restricting public worship.

Where violent opposition did take place, it was often caused by local grievances brought about by the increased intrusion of the state into local life. Popular resistance rarely had progressive intentions. Those who fought the French tended to fight out of traditional loyalties to the church or the overthrown dynasty. They did not fight out of attachment to liberal ideals or national identity.

In Germany, a group of reforming nationalists temporarily gained great influence with the Prussian court after the defeat of 1806. They said that a new liberal vision of a united Germany was essential if the French were to be expelled. They were quickly ousted, however, and only the military aspects of their reforms were used against Napoleon.

Again, those who fought Napoleon in Germany in 1813 fought from traditional backward-looking loyalties. While their actions were significant, Napoleon's defeat was probably more due to the actions of the German rulers who had defected to his enemies when the tide began to turn. Historians now conclude that his defeat was brought about by governments and states, not by popular resentment and resistance.

The effects of the Continental System on Britain

Britain responded to the Continental System with her own 'Orders in Council', forcing all neutral ships to call in at British ports and purchase a licence before trading with Europe. This high-handed approach made Britain unpopular with many continental states and actually led to a war with the USA in 1812–1814.

The effects of the system were not as great as Napoleon had supposed, because Britain was able to find new markets outside Europe, especially in South America.

You should not compare the German blockades of the two World Wars with the Continental System, for whereas the latter aimed to starve Britain of food and raw materials, Napoleon simply wanted to strip the country of its gold reserves. He was willing, therefore, to allow European merchants to sell to the British (after they had bought an expensive licence from him). This meant that during the poor harvest of 1811 Europe continued to sell grain to Britain, a move which, if it did not actually prevent famine, undoubtedly eased growing domestic political difficulties by keeping bread prices down.

The Tide Turns 1807–1809

THE CONTINENTAL SYSTEM

After Tilsit, Britain was the only state (apart from Portugal) which remained at war with Napoleon. He could not break Britain militarily, so he decided on economic action. Under his Continental System, he attempted to close Europe to British goods in the hope of driving Britain to bankruptcy. During the years 1807–1813, the British economy certainly felt the negative effects of the system, but these were never sufficient to allow Napoleon to 'conquer the sea by power of the land'. On the contrary, the system was to play a key role in his own downfall.

In attempting to close European ports to British trade, Napoleon gravely overstretched himself and increased anti-French feeling throughout the continent. The loss of British trade was economically damaging to many European states and left them with little choice but to defy the Emperor and risk his reprisals. These reprisals, though decisive, made Napoleon a number of implacable enemies. In order to enforce the system, he invaded the Papal States and imprisoned the Pope (1808), annexed Holland (deposing his brother Louis in the process) and much of the North German coastline (1810) and made an unforgiving foe of Sweden by seizing Swedish Pomerania (1811). Worse than this, the enforcement of the Continental System led Napoleon into two disastrous wars in the Iberian peninsula and Russia.

THE INVASION OF SPAIN AND PORTUGAL

In 1807 a French army under Marshal Junot was given a free passage through Spain to invade Portugal in order to enforce compliance with the Continental System. With French troops already occupying many key Spanish fortresses, Napoleon treacherously decided to conquer Spain as well as Portugal. An efficient French administration in Spain would make the country a more reliable and productive ally, and crack down on Spanish smugglers who were weakening the embargo on British goods.

In 1808 Napoleon exploited bitter divisions between Charles IV and his son Ferdinand to have both renounce the Spanish throne in favour of his own brother Joseph. An army was sent to occupy Madrid and a number of French-style reforms were announced with the intention of winning over the Spanish people. Here Napoleon seriously miscalculated, for although a small number of urban middle-class Spaniards supported his reforms, the majority of people remained loyal to the deposed Bourbons. They were willing to be led against the French by the priests and nobles who had most to lose from any reform. Within a short time of Joseph's entry into Madrid, his troops were forced into brutal repression of the population in order to maintain control. These 'Days of May' became a signal for the provinces to rise in revolt against the French. Led by regional juntas, thousands of Spanish peasants took up arms and joined guerrilla bands preying on any vulnerable French target.

The Spanish regular army was easily defeated, but it proved impossible to suppress the guerrillas, especially after the arrival of a British army under Arthur Wellesley, Duke of Wellington, in July 1808. The French were forced to fight two wars: one required the concentration of a large army to defeat the British, the other needed a diffuse presence to police the country against guerrillas. Despite having 350 000 troops in Spain, by 1814 the French were driven out and forced to defend France itself against an invading British army.

The 'Spanish ulcer' sapped Napoleon's strength and popularity. Of a total of 650 000 men who served in Spain, perhaps as many as 300 000 became casualties. His desire to wage war at the expense of the enemy was impossible to achieve in a poverty-stricken country which devoured investment for no apparent gain. What is more, continued Spanish resistance destroyed the myth of French invincibility, encouraging Napoleon's enemies elsewhere in Europe. From 1808 onwards, all French resources had to be divided between two fronts.

THE AUSTRIAN CAMPAIGN 1809

In July 1808 a Spanish regular army won a rare success over a depleted French force at Bailén. News of the victory encouraged Austria to make one more attempt to defeat Napoleon. Substantially reformed and enlarged (see Chapter 5), the Austrian army was now a much more formidable opponent than Napoleon had faced at Austerlitz. Greatly weakened, he rashly attacked the Austrians at the villages of Aspern-Essling; but his crude frontal attacks were repulsed at great cost. Although he was able to win a narrow, expensive victory at Wagram a few weeks later, he was alarmed enough to seek an alliance with Austria through marriage. Hastily divorcing Josephine, who had failed to bear him a heir, he married the Habsburg princess Marie Louise.

The whole period is briskly covered by Maurice Hutt, *Napoleon* (Oxford University Press, 1965). For specialist histories of the war in Spain and the Russian campaign, you might try M. Glover, *The Peninsular War 1807–14* (David & Charles, 1974) and A.W. Palmer, *Napoleon and Russia* (André Deutsch, 1967).

Guerrillas – combatants outside regular army units who fought using 'hit-and-run' tactics

French troops execute suspected guerrillas: a painting by the Spanish artist Goya. The war in Spain was perhaps the most vicious of the entire period. Guerrillas rarely took prisoners and often tortured French captives to death. The French responded with their own atrocities against Spanish civilians.

THE KEY ISSUE

● How important was the Russian campaign of 1812 in Napoleon's downfall?

THE KEY SKILL

Assessment

Resistance in Russia and Spain

It is very tempting to compare Russian and Spanish popular resistance to the French invaders with the nationalism that inspired the French soldiers during the revolutionary and Consular periods. However, Russian and Spanish partisans and guerrillas were not fighting for liberal or progressive ideals, such as political 'freedom' or the nation state. They fought out of traditional loyalties to monarch and church, or simply out of hatred for foreigners. As such, they opposed the values that were later to dominate Europe.

Use the following four factors in Napoleon's downfall as headings for your notes:

● Continental System
● Spain
● Russia
● Military decline.

Under each heading include the following subtitles, which will enable you to assess the significance of the factor:

● Material effects
● Diplomatic/political implications
● Can Napoleon be blamed?

Now attempt the following question: *Was Napoleon responsible for his own downfall?*

Defeat and Abdication 1810–1814

RELATIONS WITH RUSSIA

Napoleon's relations with Tsar Alexander soured quickly after Tilsit. Many in the Russian court felt cheated and angered when it became obvious that Napoleon had no intention of allowing Russia to expand at the expense of the Ottoman Empire. Their mood was not improved by his annexation of the German Duchy of Oldenburg (the dispossessed Duke was the Tsar's brother-in-law), or by his enlargement of the Duchy of Warsaw at Austrian expense after the war of 1809.

The Tsar may have felt personal affront at Napoleon's marriage to an Austrian princess in place of his own sister, but the greatest cause of discontent was probably the effect of the Continental System on the Russian economy. Russia was an important supplier of raw materials to Britain, and the loss of the British market was felt keenly by merchants and nobles alike. In December 1810 the Tsar responded to their pressure and effectively left the system by announcing that Russian ports were now open to neutral vessels. Napoleon reacted to this challenge by assembling an army for the invasion of Russia.

THE RUSSIAN DISASTER 1812

Napoleon assembled an army of 600 000 men in Poland during the summer of 1812. As usual, his plan was to seek an early and decisive battle followed by a quick peace; but as the Russians could not match the Grand Army's numbers, their only option was to deny him this opportunity by retreating and destroying everything in their path which might be of use to the enemy. The cumbersome Grand Army pursued but, ravaged by disease, hunger and desertion, was incapable of forcing a decisive engagement.

When the Russian commander Kutusov finally turned to face the French 100 miles (160 km) outside Moscow at the village of Borodino, Napoleon launched a costly frontal assault on their prepared defences. Although the attack was eventually successful, the Russians were able to retreat in good order. Napoleon now entered Moscow to find the city almost deserted. Fires were deliberately started by Russian partisans in order to deprive the French of food and shelter, and Napoleon's appeals to the Tsar to negotiate went unanswered. Isolated and facing starvation, the remnants of the Grand Army had no choice but to retreat.

With inadequate supplies, desperate winter conditions and masses of vengeful peasants and cossacks harassing the retiring columns, the retreat soon lost all semblance of order. The Russians, however, were too severely weakened to block the retreat or the entire army might have been annihilated. As it was, only 25 000 of the original core army of 400 000 crossed the Niemen into Poland in early December 1812. By then, Napoleon had long since left for Paris where he intended to deal with any possible domestic opposition and raise a new army.

LEIPZIG AND THE CAMPAIGN OF 1813

The French retreat into Germany offered a golden chance for a Fourth Coalition to unite and press their advantage. Frederick William of Prussia hesitated as usual, but his hand was forced when General Yorck, commander of a Prussian flanking force during the invasion, changed sides and joined the Russians. Prussia and Russia marched against Napoleon's hastily assembled army. In early 1813 the allies suffered two defeats, but managed to withdraw intact because the French no longer had sufficient cavalry to mount a pursuit.

In June 1813 both sides agreed to an armistice. Napoleon believed that he would benefit most by having the time to raise and train more troops, but, when the fighting began again in August, he found himself outnumbered by a coalition which now included a revitalised Austria. Although he won an immediate victory at Dresden, he was continually let down by the incompetence of his marshals, a factor exploited by the allies who would often only attack when he was not present.

At the Battle of Leipzig he was at last forced to face the entire weight of his enemies. Some 160 000 French faced double that number of Russians, Prussians, Swedes and Austrians. He attempted a fighting withdrawal, but when a bridge carrying French troops was prematurely blown, over 60 000 were left behind to surrender to the allies. The way was now clear for an invasion of France.

ABDICATION 1814

With only a small army of raw troops, Napoleon fought a brilliant campaign to defend Paris in the spring of 1814. Despite several notable successes, he found that he could not rouse the French people to any greater effort; conscription was widely avoided, imperial servants retired quietly to their estates and the Legislature at last defied him by calling for peace. His army remained in the field, but Paris surrendered without a fight on 2 April. He was forced to abdicate. Plans were made for him to retire as ruler of the small Mediterranean island of Elba, while the Bourbons were to be restored to the throne of France.

Napoleon's role in his own destruction

There are a number of obvious reasons for Napoleon's downfall. He greatly overstretched himself with his Continental System which, to be successful, required him to dominate all of mainland Europe. His ventures into Spain and Russia were both politically and militarily ill-advised. These – combined with his below-par performance as a commander, the decline of the Grand Army and the failure of a war-weary France to rally to him in 1814 – provide a reasonable explanation for his downfall.

Behind these errors, however, is the man himself. No assessment would be complete without a consideration of Napoleon's role in his own destruction. His greatest failing was his over-ambition. He didn't know where the possible stopped. His expectations became more and more unrealistic after 1807. His harsh treatment of defeated countries such as Prussia and Austria meant that they could not accept his terms. They were always waiting for the chance of revenge – which Russia offered in 1813. He was incapable of keeping a major ally like Russia by allowing it to feel any benefit of an alliance with him.

Once he had made a decision, no matter how wrong, he was completely inflexible, believing that any reversal would encourage his enemies inside and outside France. He might have withdrawn from Spain, pulled out of Russia earlier, abandoned the Continental System or accepted the allied peace terms of 1813. This might have left him on the throne. He felt certain, however, that loss of face would have meant overthrow by non-military means.

THE KEY ISSUE

● Why was Napoleon able to regain power in France in 1815?

THE KEY SKILLS

Explanation
Assessment
Chronology

The desperate tone of this letter reveals Napoleon's personal frustrations during his time on Elba:

'I have written to you frequently; I presume you have done the same, yet I have received none of your letters ... I have had no news of my son. Such conduct is very stupid and atrocious. Your apartments are waiting for you, and I look forward to seeing you in September for the vintage. No one has any right to stand in the way of your coming ... so mind you come. I am awaiting you with impatience. You are aware of all the sentiments I bear you.'

Letter from Napoleon to Marie Louise, 18 August 1814

The Return to Power

THE RULER OF ELBA

After his abdication at Fontainebleau on 6 April 1814, Napoleon was taken to Elba where he was allowed to rule. He was provided with a annual pension of 2 million francs and a small army of 700 ex-Imperial Guardsmen who volunteered to protect the island from pirates. Characteristically, he threw himself into the reform of the economy and the tiny army of his new domain, but this pastime was never going to be sufficient to satisfy him.

His stay on Elba was made deeply unhappy by the refusal of the allies to allow him any contact with his son, the King of Rome, who was now virtually an Austrian prisoner under the new title of the Duke of Reichstadt. He was alarmed by rumours of allied plans to move him from Elba to the West Indies or the isolated volcanic island of St Helena. Furthermore, allegations of cowardice in the face of angry royalist crowds following his abdication caused Napoleon great irritation. The final straw came when the Bourbons refused to pay the promised pension, leaving him to rely on the meagre resources of Elba for the upkeep of his soldiers and his small court. Other news from Europe, however, appeared to offer him hope.

FRANCE AND EUROPE 1815

Napoleon had monitored the situation on mainland Europe very carefully, and by the beginning of 1815 all the signs appeared favourable for an attempt to return to power. The allies, meeting in Vienna to redraw the map of Europe, were soon fiercely divided, the main conflict being over Poland. Russia wanted to annex all of Poland, including the territories that had belonged to Prussia prior to 1806. As compensation, Russia suggested that Prussia should be allowed to absorb all of Saxony. This proposal, however, not only threatened Austria's standing in Central Europe, but also challenged British perceptions of the balance of power. As a result of Russian intransigence, Britain and Austria signed a secret alliance. It seemed that war could break out among the allies at any moment. This was a situation that Napoleon knew only too well how to exploit.

In France, the restored Bourbons soon made themselves unpopular. Conscription and tax increases introduced by Napoleon were unexpectedly retained. Although a liberal charter guaranteed constitutional rights, rumours of the restoration of confiscated church and noble lands alienated both the middle class and the peasants. Many Frenchmen viewed the Bourbons as lackeys who 'returned in the allied baggage train'. This resentment was exacerbated by the triumphalist attitude of the new rulers with their endless religious and military parades.

The greatest resentment of all was felt by the army. In what appeared to be a calculated insult, the new king, Louis XVIII, made Dupont (the defeated commander at Bailén) Minister of War. He immediately retired thousands of officers on half-pay, their places being taken by émigré royalists who, only months before, had fought against France. The Imperial Guard all but lost its special status and was replaced with a new Royal Guard. Worse still, thousands of angry and confused demobilised soldiers were stranded with little means of survival. The feelings of the rank and file gave Napoleon real hope that they would rally to him if he returned to France.

NAPOLEON RETURNS TO FRANCE

Faced with a choice between a bleak future on Elba and the opportunity for a return to power in Europe, Napoleon could not resist the urge to try his luck one more time. On 26 February 1815 he set sail in his one ship, packed to the gunnels with the 1100 men of his personal escort. He landed at Antibes and marched for Paris. All along the route, whole army garrisons quickly abandoned their allegiance to the Bourbons and joined him. Marshal Ney (who had taken service with the Bourbons) was sent out to confront Napoleon at Lyons, but he too went over to his old commander. On hearing of Ney's defection, Louis XVIII fled, abandoning Paris to Napoleon.

He arrived in Paris to find the situation to his disadvantage. On hearing of his return, the allies had quickly patched up their differences. Napoleon's attempts to split them or buy time with offers of friendship to Britain and Austria fell on deaf ears. He was declared an international outlaw to be removed by allied military action. Before he could meet this external threat, however, he had to settle a troubled domestic scene and rally support.

The reaction of the Imperial Guard during the Bourbons' entry into Paris after the fall of Napoleon in 1814 is recorded by Chateaubriand, a moderate royalist and opponent of Napoleon:

'I suppose that such menacing and terrible impressions have never been seen on the human face. Some, wrinkling their foreheads, made their bearskins fall over their eyes to shut out the sight; some drew down the corners of their mouths in contempt and rage; others showed their teeth, through their moustaches, like tigers.'

The mood of the Grand Army in early 1815:

'... soldiers were clearly angry ... The thousands who returned from the abominable and deadly prison hulks in England were in no mood to consider the allies as liberators. The thousands of others who returned from the garrisons and fortresses of Germany, Holland and Belgium knew that no one had defeated them and believed that somehow Napoleon had been betrayed. Even defeat did not convince soldiers from Spain who marched through the streets of Grenoble shouting "Long Live the Emperor! Long Live the King of Rome!"'

D.M.G. Sutherland, France 1789–1815: Revolution and Counterrevolution, 1985

The incident at Grenoble (left), as described by Felix Markham, Napoleon and the Awakening of Europe (1958):

'When Napoleon's small force found itself faced by an infantry battalion barring the road, Napoleon took one of the boldest decisions of his career. He ordered his men to put their muskets under their arms, and advancing alone in his familiar grey overcoat, he shouted: "Kill your Emperor, if you wish." Ignoring all commands to fire, the battalion broke ranks, and surrounded Napoleon with shouts of "Vive l'Empereur".'

THE KEY ISSUES

- Did Napoleon become a genuine liberal in 1815?
- What is the significance of the Hundred Days?

THE KEY SKILL

Assessment

You probably won't get a question solely on the Hundred Days in the exam. This topic may, however, reinforce knowledge of Napoleon from other Key Issues, such as:

- Napoleon as a commander
- Napoleon's political opinions
- Napoleon's legend.

For note headings you might consider:

- Why was Napoleon able to return to power?
- Why did Napoleon introduce liberal reforms in France?
- Was Napoleon doomed from the very start of the Hundred Days?

The threat from abroad:

'Europe was about to come down on France like an avalanche. She had from 700 000 to 800 000 men on foot, considerable reserves, and all the resources of England at her disposal.'

George Lefebvre, Napoleon, 1969

The Final Defeat

THE LIBERAL EMPIRE

By the time he reached Lyons, Napoleon had realised that, in the excitement at his return, political life in France had revived. In particular, extreme Jacobinism re-emerged in many French cities as the middle class sought revenge on the resurgent nobility and church. Napoleon had no taste for Jacobin politics, but he was determined to play on these sentiments to win support. He began a series of violent verbal attacks on the clergy and the aristocrats, threatening to 'string them up from the lamp-posts'. He followed this with an Additional Act to the constitution, ensuring universal suffrage, freedom of the press and ministers who were responsible to the elected chambers. Predictably, the Additional Act was confirmed with a plebiscite which yielded 1 552 942 votes in favour and 5740 against. The most notable feature of the result was that only one in five of the electorate bothered to vote.

Napoleon's liberal measures did not result from a transformation in his political beliefs, but rather from a cynical attempt to win popularity. He himself later admitted that he viewed the Additional Act as a temporary expedient which would be abolished when circumstances were favourable. Despite this gesture, the liberals remained understandably suspicious of his intentions. Throughout the Hundred Days of his new regime, his main support seems to have come from the peasants, who viewed him as the guarantor of the land settlement, and from the army, whose soldiers had suffered so much at the hands of the Bourbons.

PREPARATIONS FOR WAR

Napoleon could not spend long on domestic problems: the threat from abroad was too great. By the late spring of 1815, a British army under Wellington, supplemented by Dutch and Belgian contingents, was assembling in Belgium with plans to link with a Prussian force under Gerbhard von Blücher. Behind them, Austria and Russia were mobilising in strength. As in the campaign of 1805, Napoleon realised the danger of allowing these allied armies the time to unite. He needed a quick victory, either to split the coalition or force the allies to negotiate.

His attempts to organise an army were severely hampered by a lack of money and draft horses. Although he was helped by the return of prisoners of war, it was difficult to raise large numbers of troops because, right up until the start of June, he didn't dare resort to conscription. Of the 300 000 men who were eventually raised, many had to be used for border guard duties and internal policing against royalist uprisings. This left him with a striking force of 120 000 – with which he unexpectedly marched into Belgium on 14 June 1815.

THE WATERLOO CAMPAIGN

Napoleon's intention was to prevent Wellington's 90 000 men from linking up with Blücher's army of 120 000, so that he could defeat them separately. He almost succeeded. On 16 June he defeated Blücher's army at Ligny, although the Prussians were able to retire in good order because no enveloping force arrived. Meanwhile, 7 miles (11 km) away at Quatre Bras, Ney prevented Wellington from intervening.

The French now turned on Wellington who had retired to Waterloo following the inconclusive engagement at Quatre Bras. Napoleon mistakenly believed that the Prussians were no longer a threat, so he sent Marshal Grouchy after them with an army of 30 000 men. Grouchy never found Blücher, who had kept in close contact with Wellington and was marching to join him at Waterloo.

The Battle of Waterloo, fought on 18 June 1815, was characterised by Napoleon's lack of energy and Ney's impetuous poor judgement. Rather than attempt any sort of manoeuvre, Napoleon simply planned to smash through the centre of Wellington's line using massed columns. When his plan was questioned by those present who had witnessed the steadiness of the British infantry in Spain, he swept their objections aside. He then passed tactical control of the battle over to Ney, who ordered a series of costly frontal attacks by infantry and unsupported cavalry. These crude French tactics almost succeeded; but when the Prussians unexpectedly arrived and attacked the French flank, Napoleon's army was routed.

Napoleon hurried back to Paris in the hope of raising yet another army, but this time the politicians refused to be cowed into obedience. Napoleon was forced to abdicate for a second time on 22 June. He fled to the coast, hoping to escape to America or retire to England; but instead he was exiled to St Helena in the South Atlantic.

A British officer appeals to the Old Guard to surrender at Waterloo. Many Guard units fought almost to the last man.

The real significance of the Hundred Days

The significance of the Hundred Days has probably been exaggerated, particularly by British historians who have been keen to overstate the importance of Waterloo. It seems likely that, even had Napoleon won a crushing victory at Waterloo, he would still have faced ultimate defeat at the hands of the Russians and Austrians.

Yet the Hundred Days is significant for three reasons:

1. The first peace settlement of 1814 was very generous to France, but after the Hundred Days the new terms were much more harsh.

2. The upsurge in republicanism during the Hundred Days exacerbated political and social divisions within France, leading to a near civil war when the Bourbons were restored in 1815. The bitterness of this division was felt long afterwards.

3. Napoleon and his supporters subsequently used the Additional Act as evidence of his liberalism. This was to play a big part in the Napoleonic legend and was used to obscure the reality of his dictatorship.

Was Napoleon's return to power during the Hundred Days anything more than a military coup d'état? **?** Remember, to answer this question you will have to consider first of all the importance, and the source, of military grievances, and then look at the other contributing factors, such as the role of the Bourbons, émigrés and the church in causing middle-class and peasant anxiety.

THE KEY ISSUE

● Where did the legend of Napoleon originate?

THE KEY SKILLS

Explanation
Empathy
Assessment

What happened to ...?

Josephine Beauharnais
Napoleon remained on good terms with his former wife right up until her death in 1814.

Marie Louise
Napoleon's second wife made little effort to join him in exile. Seduced by an Austrian count, she had two children by him before Napoleon's death. She was made ruler of Tuscany.

The King of Rome
Napoleon's young son had a short, tragic life. Brought up as an Austrian prince under the title of the Duke of Reichstadt, he was encouraged to forget his past, but at the same time was a virtual outcast at the Austrian court. He died of tuberculosis in 1832.

Marshal Ney
Ney agreed to serve the restored Bourbons, but returned to Napoleon during the Hundred Days. He was shot by firing squad in 1815.

Joachim Murat
He was executed after an abortive attempt to regain power in Naples.

A Legend in Life

NAPOLEON ON ST HELENA 1815–1821

Predictably, Napoleon's time on St Helena was unhappy. He was guarded by no fewer than 3000 troops, and a number of warships patrolled the offshore waters. Despite this, the governor of the island, Sir Hudson Lowe, lived in constant fear of an escape attempt. The last six years of Napoleon's life were spent in petty quarrels with Lowe, whose vindictiveness extended to refusing Napoleon the right to the title of ex-Emperor, cutting his household budget and restricting his movements about the island. British precautions were unnecessary, for there is no evidence that a bid for freedom was ever seriously contemplated. Instead, Napoleon used Lowe's tactlessness for his own propaganda purposes: he was determined to be awkward, believing that 'the more I am persecuted, the more noise it will make in Europe'.

Soon after arriving on St Helena, Napoleon's health began to suffer. Although the climate was not particularly unhealthy, a virus-infested water supply made liver disease a frequent killer. For several years his health complaints were treated as hypochondria by the British who were convinced that he was simply out to embarrass them.

Napoleon in the garden of Longwood, his home on St Helena, 1815

When, in 1820, his health deteriorated to a life-threatening degree, they were keen to avoid the verdict of liver disease. If death were judged to have been hastened by conditions during his imprisonment, Napoleon would become a martyr and his gaolers culpable. When he died on 5 May 1821, a British naval surgeon who was so bold as to claim that Napoleon had suffered from liver disease was cashiered from the service; and Napoleon's own surgeon refused to sign the official autopsy report which gave stomach cancer as the cause of death.

THE LIVING LEGEND

During his time in power, Napoleon was always conscious of his image. His propaganda was delivered by every means available at the time, and he sought to use the teacher and the priest to influence the young and the illiterate. All this effort was not simply to serve an immediate political purpose – Napoleon nurtured a keen sense of his own greatness which he was determined to proclaim to future generations. He indulged in fantasies, comparing himself with past figures from ancient and medieval history. When he was in Egypt, he saw himself as a new Alexander the Great, sweeping aside eastern empires on his way to India (which was conveniently a precious British possession). Later, he thought of himself as a Roman Caesar, dispensing law and military glory in equal measure to the French people. His last and most pervasive persona was Charlemagne, the great medieval emperor who had christianised much of Europe. Napoleon's choice of Charlemagne coincided with his own self-proclaimed role as a pan-European ruler spreading a gospel of enlightened government.

Napoleon as a French Caesar in a triumphal procession

THE LEGEND OF THE HUNDRED DAYS AND ST HELENA

Napoleon's failure during the Hundred Days added tragic romance to his popular image. Furthermore, his liberal additions to the old Napoleonic constitution allowed him to add the mantle of liberator to that of unrivalled military genius and omniscient administrator. Historians have claimed, perhaps rightly, that Napoleon's legend was sealed by his ultimate fate as a lonely exile on a remote island. Had he been granted his wish and allowed a comfortable retirement in England or the United States, he would have been seen as nothing more than a failed and flawed human being on public display. Instead, his isolation and the exotic location of his exile added mystery and tragedy to his failure, ensuring that he was never truly forgotten while alive.

The remaining six years of his life were spent in self-justification. He took a small staff with him into exile and he let them know that by recording his thoughts for a broader audience, they could make their fortunes back in Europe. He no doubt intended to counter much of the negative propaganda being circulated by his enemies at the time. However, when Barry O'Meara (1821) and Emmanuel de Las Cases (1823) published their accounts of his ideas, they went much further and started a legend which rewrote the history of Napoleon's era.

THE KEY ISSUES

- Why is the legend of Napoleon important?
- Is there any truth in the legend?

THE KEY SKILLS

Explanation
Assessment

'I desire that my ashes repose on the banks of the Seine, in the midst of the French people whom I have loved so dearly ... I die prematurely, murdered by the English oligarchy and its hired assassin. The English people will not be slow to avenge me ... I urge my son never to forget that he was born a French prince, and never to lend himself to being an instrument in the hands of the powers who are oppressing the peoples of Europe.'

From Napoleon's will, April 1821

Oligarchy – government by a small élite class

A Legend in Death

THE NATURE OF THE LEGEND

Napoleon seems to have spent much of his time on St Helena twisting the story of his life into a form that made him a faultless martyr and excused his most unjustifiable actions. His dictatorship in France was a temporary expedient made necessary to prevent anarchy and civil war. His harsh treatment of much of Europe was forced upon him by the threat posed by the allies. He had cleared the continent of the last vestiges of feudalism, and brought justice and equality. It was because of this that he was forced to fight continual wars of self-defence against the powers who were determined to thrust the continent back into the unenlightened past.

According to the legend, his intentions hinged on the Russian campaign of 1812. Rather than being a war of aggrandisement, this was a defensive campaign aimed at winning a final peace by removing England's last ally from continental Europe. A victory in 1812 would have seen a new Napoleonic Empire based on the right of each nationality, such as the Poles, Germans or Italians, to form their own independent states. After this process, his visions for Europe became even grander. A Europe of free nation states would live in peace, and might even one day become a single people.

Napoleon's tomb in the crypt of Les Invalides in Paris. He was originally buried on St Helena where, owing to an argument between the British and the French on the island, no inscription was placed on his tomb. With British permission, his body was exhumed and transported to Paris in 1840. Its return breathed new life into the legend.

THE LATER LEGEND

That the legend endured after Napoleon's death is testimony to the power of its romance and its continuing political relevance to a troubled France. To the generation born after 1815, Napoleon appeared a great French patriot. His romantic appeal contrasted with the dull character of existing governments. Young men who heard tales from surviving veterans heard nothing of conscription and carnage on the battlefield, but only of glory and adventure.

The legend of Napoleon also appealed on a practical level. In a poorly governed France wracked by bitter social and political problems, the Napoleon of legend appeared to have reconciled all divisions. He alone established the rule of law and the sanctity of property, while remaining true to the ideals of the Revolution and showing compassion for the poor. The greatest victim and beneficiary of this illusion was Napoleon's nephew, Louis Napoleon, who, at a time of great unrest in 1848, was able to use the power of his name to be elected President. Later, he too staged a coup d'état. He declared himself Emperor of a regime which attempted to live the Napoleonic legend in all its symbols and policies. Some historians assert that the legend of Napoleon as the strongman restoring order led to a series of imitators who shaped French political life into the present century.

In the 20th century the Napoleon of legend retains a fascination for historians. Everything from his sexuality to the manner of his death has received detailed treatment. Even today the legend persists as a challenge to students of history determined to find the real Napoleon among the many enduring myths.

Andrina Stiles, *Napoleon and Europe* (Hodder & Stoughton, 1993) gives the most thorough treatment of the myth. See also Felix Markham, *Napoleon* (Weidenfeld & Nicolson, 1963).

You are unlikely to get a question in an A-level examination solely on the legend. If you do choose to make notes on this topic, you would probably be best concentrating on the content of the legend. The contrast between legend and reality is the premise for many of the examiners' questions.

If you want an activity, try refuting Napoleon's statements in the box on the (below,left).

The legend according to Napoleon

Napoleon's wars:

'The vulgar have never ceased blaming all my wars on my ambitions. But were they of my choosing? Were they not always determined by the nature of things, by the struggle between the past and the future, by the permanent coalition of our enemies, who put upon us the obligation of destroying them lest we ourselves be destroyed?'

Napoleon and the nations:

'There are in Europe more than 30 million French, 15 million Spanish, 15 million Italians, 30 million Germans. I would have wished to make each of these peoples a single united body.'

Napoleon and Europe:

'Europe thus divided into nationalities freely formed and free internally, peace between states would have become easier: the United States of Europe would have become a possibility.'

'I wish to found a European system, a European Code of Laws, a European judiciary; there would be but one people in Europe.'

Napoleon and the legend:

'I have no fear whatever about my fame. Posterity will do me justice. Had I succeeded I should have died with the reputation of the greatest man who ever existed. As it is, though I have failed I shall be considered an extraordinary man ... The historian of the Empire will have an easy task, for the facts shine like the sun ... on what point could I be assailed on which a historian could not defend me?'

A *synthesis* is a final judgement reached when all the available theories and factors concerning any issue have been considered. It might be composed largely of one theory which overpowers all the others, or it might be a combination of several different interpretations. This chapter attempts to establish four syntheses for the four Key Issues outlined at the start of the book.

This section, therefore, reflects the three stages of the A-level process:

1. I have considered the questions posed throughout the book;
2. I have weighed up all the evidence; and
3. I have come to the conclusions presented here.

This is what a synthesis should be – not just the acquisition of a lot of knowledge, but a critical understanding of the concepts and issues underlying that knowledge. Only when you can synthesise a topic can you really claim to understand it.

Furthermore, the process of synthesising any topic is a crucial life skill which makes History a vital and relevant subject in the educational curriculum.

Synthesis

1. Did Napoleon Betray the Revolution?

The Revolution went through several different phases in the ten years after 1789. It began as a liberating movement, but under the pressures of war and the leadership of the Jacobins it had become much more authoritarian by 1793–1794. Military victory brought more relaxed and less idealistic government in the form of the Directory after 1795. Such changes make it very difficult to interpret Napoleon's regime in the light of the practical actions of the revolutionaries, who themselves differed so much in policy and outlook. It is much easier to compare his domestic rule with the broad ideals of the Revolution rather than with its practical application.

It cannot seriously be claimed that Napoleon gave France liberty. His was a police state riddled with spies and informers, where freedom of expression was severely restricted and the normal process of law was suspended for those who threatened the regime. Obviously, it is easy to over-state the efficiency of these restrictions. Napoleon did not have the bureaucracy or the technology of a 20th-century dictator at his disposal. Nevertheless, his goal was clear: he wanted the complete elimination of all opposition.

He did not provide France with representative government. The complex arrangements for the selection and operation of assemblies were nothing more than a deliberate smoke screen to hide one-man rule. On the local level, his assumption of the right of appointment of local officials destroyed popular representation. He claimed that he represented the will of the French people and, despite the very dubious evidence of the four plebiscites held during his reign, there may be something in this. Many of his measures were undeniably popular, but his idea of 'representation' was not to ask people what they wanted, but to give them what he thought they wanted.

Napoleon did provide France with a limited form of 'equality'. The Code Napoléon and the Organic Articles are clear evidence of this, but equality was only granted when it did not threaten the power of his regime or his own personal prejudices. Above all, his aim was to use reform to purchase the loyalty of a small élite, while doing nothing more than ease the discontent of the majority. For Napoleon (and for most revolutionaries) equality meant the rise of middle-class men of talent; it did not extend to the lower classes and women. For the most part, he can be excused on this point, for he was after all a product of his own times. To judge him too harshly would be to apply modern value judgements to a late 18th-/early 19th-century man.

Despite the more excessive aspects of the Code Napoléon, his government was undoubtedly enlightened in some respects, and some of his reforms established in law the most common-sense aspects of the Revolution. His motivation was not enlightened, however, and it was not necessarily in the interests of the French people who, with the approach of defeat, faced tax rises and merciless conscription.

Napoleon established the revolutionary principles that would help maintain him in power by pacifying domestic opinion. Where the spirit of the Revolution went against his own interests his adherence was purely cosmetic.

2. WHY WAS NAPOLEON ABLE TO CONQUER EUROPE?

The astonishing speed of Napoleon's conquest of Europe between 1805 and 1807 has long encouraged the notion that he was an extraordinary commander who won victory after victory by the power of his unique military genius. In some respects he was an exceptional soldier, and he was certainly superior to the generals who opposed him during these years; but to put the victories down to the role of one man would be to believe Napoleon's own propaganda. Other much broader factors placed enormous power in the hands of a very ambitious man. It is his use of advantages not of his own making which made victory possible.

It is often said that the Revolution released huge nationalist energies which Napoleon was able to employ to decisive effect in the early campaigns. This may be true, but perhaps more significant is the fact the Revolution placed enormous powers in the hands of government. It was this that Napoleon really exploited to his advantage. The power that he enjoyed over French subjects was unrivalled by his enemies. The efficiency of the French state gave it the edge over unreformed states such as Prussia and Austria.

At the same time, the incompetence and inflexibility of his enemies, who fought with woefully outmoded tactics and could achieve neither military nor diplomatic coordination, must feature prominently in any explanation of French success.

A purely military interpretation, in which the new tactics of the Grand Army and the ingenious strategies of its commander bring victory over inferior enemies, is not completely satisfying. The roots of French triumph lie with the Revolution, not with Napoleon. French social, military and administrative development left its enemies far behind in the 1790s, and French victories up to 1807 were nothing more than conclusive evidence of this fact.

Arriving at your own synthesis

Read the syntheses in this chapter carefully ... what if you don't agree with them?

Well, the answer to that one is simple: make your own! My syntheses are just that ... mine. If you don't like them, it doesn't mean that they are wrong; but it does mean that you need to create your own to put in their place.

Everyone who studies Napoleon will have a different view of the man and his achievements. That's part of the reason why it is so important to read as widely as possible. If you read only one author, you run the risk of becoming the slave of his or her opinions. To form your own synthesis you must read widely.

'The lay state, religious toleration, equality before the law, the absence of exemptions from taxation and from the ordinary obligations of citizens, careers open to talent, conscript armies, logical, instead of traditional, administrative organisation, professional bureaucracy, and the basic concept of the utilitarian ends of government. This is what Bonaparte gave to France – or rather, preserved to France out of the revolutionary heritage – and offered to Europe.'

J. McManners, Lectures on European History 1789-1914, 1974

The legacy of Napoleon

Consider carefully each of the principles listed in the box above which Napoleon bequeathed to France. Do you feel that Napoleon delivered them in practice? Is it more important for the future that some of them were 'established' in theory by Napoleon than that he actually observed them in reality?

3. WHAT BROUGHT ABOUT NAPOLEON'S DOWNFALL?

The path to Napoleon's downfall is littered with significant milestones: the introduction of the Continental System by which he overstretched himself and alienated much of Europe; the occupation of Spain which slowly bled the Empire dry; the invasion of Russia which destroyed the Grand Army and provided the opportunity for his enemies to unite against him; and the mistakes of the 1813–1814 campaigns in Germany.

Each event is certainly significant, and it is the happy pastime of examiners to ask students to compare their importance. But they cannot be seen in isolation. The Continental System roused parts of Europe against Napoleon and led directly to his invasion of Spain, Portugal and Russia. Had he not been over-committed in Spain, he might have been able to pacify his eastern enemies. And had he not had to challenge Russia in 1812, he might have been able to crush the Spaniards and drive the British out of the Iberian peninsula.

It is too easy to turn events after 1807 into a simple equation which adds up to Napoleon's downfall. Other less tangible factors must be considered. It might be said that Napoleon rose on the wave of energy and imagination created by the Revolution, and that once that energy faded he was bound to decline. The dilution of the Grand Army – from a national force defending France from invasion to a multi-national army operating aggressively (for no obviously legitimate reason) well beyond the borders of France – provides a good illustration of this decline. So, too, does the indifference of Paris when threatened by foreign armies in 1814. It is perhaps satisfying to suggest that Napoleon's cynical exploitation of revolutionary ideals created a similar cynicism within French society which then lost the desire for victory.

Another valid interpretation is that Napoleon was destroyed by the very forces that created him. Just as he harnessed the emotional nationalism of the French, so he was later challenged by emotional reactions from the peoples of Germany, Spain and Russia. In Germany, this took the form of recognisably modern nationalism; but elsewhere it was a reaction against modernity that drove Napoleon's opponents to rally round the *ancien régime*.

France did not simply lose the edge in emotional terms – its superiority was worn away by practical improvements made by its enemies. The scale of French victories led to practical reforms in every state threatened by Napoleon. Military reforms were important, but so too were the modern administrative changes carried out in countries such as Austria and Prussia. Napoleon's enemies learned their lesson from defeat and quickly narrowed the gap on France.

Whatever the significance of individual events, it is important that we see them as a whole, and not as isolated occurrences. It is also important that we trace each event back to its single root, Napoleon himself. He fell from power as a result of his own mistakes. He recognised no limits on his ambition. After 1807 his plans became more grandiose and unrealistic. His enemies realised that he could not be dealt with by diplomatic means. He had to be stopped.

4. NAPOLEON'S EUROPE: LIBERATION OR EXPLOITATION?

The Empire lasted such a short time and was constantly at war: these two factors make it difficult to judge Napoleon's ultimate intentions. The obvious interpretation is that the Empire was set up simply to facilitate the exploitation of its peoples and turn their resources against the enemies of France. As such, it was formed through a series of expedients with no overall plan or philosophy behind its construction. Many of the later theories were simply grafted on by Napoleon or his supporters who, given the value of hindsight, realised what image would play well with a European audience after 1815.

In reality, Napoleon viewed reform as a practical proposition. He felt that he had pacified France by giving most Frenchmen what they wanted. His reforms throughout the Empire were aimed at repeating this trick on a continental scale. Whatever his intentions, the Empire did stimulate nationalism in Italy and Germany, and did give encouragement to liberalism across Europe. But this was as much a reaction to imperial repression as it was a response to progressive reform.

Napoleon undoubtedly challenged the old élite in many parts of Europe, but he did not set out to spark a social revolution. Existing élites were only attacked where they were unwilling to collaborate. Had the Empire lasted much longer, Napoleon may well have favoured a European superstate ruled from Paris; but the model for such a state would have looked back to ancient Rome, not forward to a modern union of free states.

Napoleon on Napoleon

'People will wonder whether or not I really aimed at universal monarchy. It will be argued at length whether my absolute authority and my arbitrary actions were the effects of my character or my calculations; whether they were the results of my inclinations or of the force of circumstance; whether my unending wars were caused by my enjoying them or whether I was pushed into them against my will; whether the driving force behind my immense ambition ... was lust for power or thirst for glory, the necessity of establishing order or the desire to promote men's welfare – for the question deserves to be examined from several different points of view.'

Two historians on Napoleon:

'With all his intelligence, Bonaparte had no significant vision of the future.'

J. McManners, Lectures on European History 1789–1914, 1974

'The Empire was to endure only ten years, but the ideas behind it were to survive down to the present day.'

Vincent Cronin, Napoleon, 1971

Napoleon as the prophet of a new age

Look at the two ideas expressed by the historians in the box on the left, and Napoleon's own account. Is it possible to synthesise them? Do Napoleon's actions show a lack of foresight? Were they dominated by the past rather than by a vision of the future? Is it possible that he shaped the future without having any idea of what that future might be?

Argument

QUESTIONS ABOUT NAPOLEON'S DOMESTIC POLICIES

Napoleon's domestic policies feature regularly in A-level exam papers. Examiners often base their question around the nature of Napoleon's regime and the apparent contradiction of an authoritarian dictatorship which claimed to be inspired by the ideals of a libertarian revolution.

Questions which ask about his relationship to the Revolution, the lack of opposition to his regime or the factors that kept him in power all spring from the same controversy. In different ways and with different wording, they are all asking you to strike an informed balance between the image of Napoleon as a repressive dictator and the idea that for many people his regime existed because it met their social, political and economic needs.

Predictably, the answer does lie in the balance and you may choose to lean either way, but you must demonstrate an awareness of the validity of each case before coming to your conclusion.

You should be aware of the repressive element, including the sham of representative government (and how it was achieved), the police, spies, censorship, politicised legal system and the power of the Prefects. You must be able to balance these factors with those reforms that clearly owe a debt to the Revolution (and were therefore popular), including the Code Napoléon, the Concordat and, to a lesser extent, the education reforms.

Additionally, in questions that relate to Napoleon's hold on power, his supporters or his opponents, you will need an awareness of the more practical measures that he took to attract supporters. You must know about his use of propaganda, the awards of government posts, grants of land and money, and the nature and purpose of the Legion of Honour and the imperial nobility.

In this type of essay your conclusion should be used to balance the different features of Napoleon's regime. All dictatorships use 'carrots and sticks', and, as long as you show that you are aware of this, you may lean either way. Remember, authoritarian government is always unpopular. After the chaos and lawlessness of the Revolution, there were probably many people in France who welcomed a strong regime which would enforce order and guarantee property, even at the expense of liberty.

1. Who supported Napoleon within France?

The key to this question is to be specific. Don't attempt to provide a general treatment which may leave important factors out altogether. Instead you must identify each group (preferably within your introduction) and explain how Napoleon's policies might have led them to support him, or at least to offer no real opposition to his rule.

Start at the top with the élite self-seeking group of commanders and administrators who benefited from his largesse in terms of titles, enhanced career opportunities and wealth. You might also wish to discuss Napoleon's standing with the ordinary rank-and-file of the army.

You can then describe how his policies positively affected the middle class, urban workers and peasants. Each group might have a paragraph to itself. Thus the essay would have an easy and obvious structure.

Your conclusion should point out who benefited most from Napoleon's rule. You should be able to provide a discerning judgement of which groups genuinely supported him and which were merely pacified or appeased into acceptance.

2. Which of Napoleon's domestic reforms was the most successful?

Your introduction should outline the list of reforms which you will use as the subject of each following paragraph. In order to provide an adequate answer you must define 'success'. For our purpose, this will be the reform that best met the need for which it was created.

The two big reforms that should be handled first are the Code Napoléon and the Concordat. Describe the circumstances that created the need for action in each case, then discuss whether the reform itself met its original aims. Remember, this aim may not be what you would expect. For example, the Concordat was not simply about clarifying the position of the Catholic church; it was also meant to make the church an active arm of Napoleon's regime.

Deal next with the lesser reforms such as the Bank of France and the *lycées*, remembering that the success of any reform must also be judged by the difficulty of its imposition. Although the lesser reforms were successful, you must show that they were less controversial and more limited in their original aims.

Conclude by outlining how each reform was successful. You may wish to choose one particular measure, or you may argue that some have equal significance.

Timing is everything

The time that you might have to answer an exam question will vary depending on the exam board, but average times range from 45 minutes to one hour. This means that the first thing you need to be able to do is organise your time properly.

If you are in an exam in which you must write more than one essay you must split your time evenly between them. All too often a candidate will find one essay going particularly well and decide to spend more time on it at the expense of a later essay. Don't do it! You will find that the marks lost on the later essay are not made up by the time spent on earlier work. Remember, two moderate essay marks will total up to more than one very good mark.

Time is limited in an exam, so you must not waste it. But this does not mean that you should tear into the first question that looks familiar because you want to write as much as possible. You must read all the relevant questions and choose carefully. Too many students get half-way through a question only to realise that they have misread it and no longer feel competent to provide an answer.

Once you have chosen your question, it is absolutely vital that you take the time to write some sort of plan before you start to write the body of the essay.

Planning your exam essay

Too many students think that planning an exam essay is a waste of time, yet it is vital if you are to achieve a good final mark.

Not only is it an invaluable aid in structuring your answer, but it may also save you time in the long run. If you have a series of signposts written down beforehand, you won't get lost and have to spend time remembering the point of your argument.

The few minutes you spend planning is the most important time in the writing of an essay. It is your opportunity to get an overview of the whole question before delving into the detail where you might get lost. The only other opportunity you will get will come when you write your conclusion, and by then it may be too late.

You probably don't need to spend a long time on a plan – it does not have to make sense to anyone but you! You might simply write it as a list with a few catch-phrases attached to jog your memory, or you may decide that it is worth more time. That is up to you. But you will only find out through practice. You must use whichever type of plan works best for you, but you *must* use a plan of some sort.

QUESTIONS ABOUT NAPOLEON'S CONQUEST OF EUROPE AND DOWNFALL

The circumstances and factors that led to Napoleon's downfall are frequently visited by examiners. There are a number of factors, and examiners often ask students to compare the importance of one with all the others. This is not really such a difficult question. It draws on a limited body of information and tests your ability to tailor your knowledge to meet a specific 'slant'.

The obvious factors that you must consider in Napoleon's downfall include the role of the Continental System, the war in Spain and the Russian campaign. To these must be added other factors, such as the growth of nationalism throughout Europe and, crucially, Napoleon's own personal faults and mistakes.

You must begin by showing a thorough awareness of the significance of the event or factor mentioned in the question. Only then can you branch out into a discussion of the other factors and their relative merits. Each other factor might have a paragraph of its own, but you should bear in mind that the highest marks will go to the candidate who can resist the urge to see the factors in separate compartments, but is able to show the links between them.

Questions on Napoleon's conquest of Europe are slightly less popular than those on his downfall, but still make regular appearances on exam papers. In this case the key controversy might centre around an assessment of the personal contribution of Napoleon or a comparison of French advantages with allied disadvantages.

When assessing the role of Napoleon, you must obviously consider his contribution as a decisive commander. However, you must also compare this to the other broader factors that he either had no control over (such as the disadvantages and incompetence of his enemies) or did little to create (the splendid bureaucratic and military machine that he inherited from the Revolution). Achieving an informed balance between the two should deliver a good exam result.

If you are asked to compare the strength of France with the weakness of its enemies you should divide your time equally between a consideration of the two. Your conclusion should show an awareness that strength and weakness are relative and that neither can be considered in isolation.

3. Did Britain make the greatest contribution to Napoleon's downfall?

It is easy to fall into the trap of thinking that this question is solely about Britain. In reality, it is much broader because in order to provide a satisfactory answer you need to compare the role of Britain with that of all the other states that were active in Napoleon's downfall.

Start with a thorough discussion of Britain's role. Include diplomatic and financial efforts in forming the coalitions. Consider the constant naval threat to the European coastline and the psychological impact of the military effort in Spain. Discuss Britain's part in provoking the disastrous Continental System. Britain was certainly significant, but what about the other states?

Write a series of short paragraphs showing the importance of Spain, Russia, Austria and Prussia in Napoleon's downfall and comparing them with Britain's contribution.

The tone that you adopt in this essay is a matter of choice and personal opinion. You may wish to attack the notion that Britain was very important by stressing the role of the other powers who certainly suffered much more in human terms; or you may wish to take the opposite line and argue that resistance in Europe would have collapsed without constant British encouragement. You may even choose a more sophisticated line and point out that all the powers contributed something quite different and that it was their combined resistance that brought Napoleon down.

4. 'Borodino marks the turning-point in Napoleon's bid to conquer Europe.' Do you agree?

This question is basically about the comparison of sudden and dramatic events with more gradual trends. You must demonstrate not simply an awareness of the significance of Borodino and the Russian campaign in general, but you must also show an understanding of the long-term trends that occurred before and after the 'big event' – and which are probably more important.

Begin with a full description of the importance and consequences of Borodino and the Russian campaign.

Discuss the possibility that Napoleon's fortunes were already on the turn long before Borodino, what with the Continental System, the war in Spain and the revival of states like Prussia and Austria which were awaiting an opportunity for revenge.

Consider the possibility that even after Borodino Napoleon may still have reversed his unfavourable situation during 1813–1815.

Introducing your essay

Even in the limited time available in an exam, every essay should have an introduction. Below are the beginnings of two poor introductions:

'In 1808, Napoleon was at the height of his powers. All Europe quaked at his feet. Only plucky Britain denied his insane quest for world domination.'

'Napoleon betrayed the Revolution. He made himself a dictator and took away the liberties of the French people.'

The first introduction is a piece of flowery writing which does nothing to begin any serious answer. The second is a conclusion which seems to assert an opinion before it has received detailed support from the body of an essay. These two constitute the most common misconceptions about the nature and purpose of an introduction.

In reality, an introduction is essential because it steers the rest of the essay. It is a practical and purposeful piece of writing which outlines the issues that need to be discussed in the body of the essay and defines the terms of reference of the entire piece. It should not pre-judge your conclusion by asserting opinions; instead, it should describe the possible interpretations which are to be discussed later.

The secret of writing a good essay is to attempt to answer the question. This is not as easy as it sounds. Most students who don't make a plan will inevitably gravitate towards telling the story as they know it, rather than providing a direct answer.

Set out to make perhaps four or five points, each of which, when combined with supporting evidence, will compose a paragraph. By planning your essay around points you will be able to avoid the temptation to fall back on the story.

Remember that you must support each point with evidence, otherwise you will be making unsupported assertions which attract the disapproval of examiners. At the same time, you should be careful not to swamp your points in evidence. Select the evidence which is most conclusive or typical and which can be expressed most succinctly so as to allow you maximum time for interpretation.

If you have planned and structured your essay properly, the conclusion should be very straightforward. A good conclusion can be written by re-reading the essay. Consult the issues raised in your introduction and then refer to each point that you develop in the body of the essay. Then express your overall opinion.

Never introduce new material in a conclusion – and remember, a good conclusion drives up marks.

OTHER QUESTIONS ABOUT NAPOLEON

After you have covered Napoleon's rule in France, his conquest of Europe and his downfall, there are a number of less popular areas which sometimes appear in exam papers.

Napoleon's Europe appears with some frequency. The questions usually revolve around his intentions in forming the Empire, and you may be asked to compare his claims about the nationalities, universal empire or liberalism within the Empire with the reality of his ruthless exploitation and cynical disregard for the will of those he ruled.

His rise to power may also feature. In this case the tendency may be to contrast the role of his own actions and merits with the broader factors that he did not control. He was undoubtedly a product of the Revolution and the opportunities and chaos that it brought. It might even be argued that had Bonaparte not seized power, some other military strongman would have taken his place. Yet Napoleon did have extraordinary military and civil qualities. His regime was not secure until after 1800, and you might stress that it was the way in which he managed to retain power rather than his rise that marks him out as exceptional.

Napoleon as a military commander still exercises some attraction for examiners, especially as it is a debate enlivened by recent and belated criticism from historians. Again, the basic division is between those who see his victories as the product of individual genius and those who believe that they were brought about by more general military, political and social advantages which he was fortunate to inherit from the Revolution and the years of warfare which preceded his coup.

Where the Hundred Days feature as an exam question, it may possibly focus on the reasons why Napoleon was able to return to power. There are two obvious aspects to this. First, the gross mistakes and insensitivity of the Bourbons and the émigrés which made them immediately unpopular with much of the population. Second, the appeal of Napoleon. You must be careful in such a question not to give a general treatment of French public opinion at the time. Napoleon's appeal was much greater with certain sections of society (and particularly the army) than with others who remained indifferent to his return.

The supposed enthusiasm that greeted his return in 1815 may be contrasted with the indifference to his departure in the previous year. To explain the contrast, you will need to consider in particular the role of the Bourbons and of the thousands of soldiers who returned to France at the end of hostilities in 1814.

5. To what extent did Napoleon benefit the people of Europe?

Napoleon's immediate goal was obviously not to benefit the people of Europe, but you must demonstrate balance in this essay. You should begin by outlining the possible benefits, but also allude to the cost of Napoleon's rule. Then the body of your essay will deal with each in turn.

Describe the benefits of his rule. Include the abolition of feudalism, the removal of the arbitrary rule of old monarchs and the destruction of church privilege. You must balance this, however, with a critical analysis of the limitations of reform. The abolition of feudalism was not a complete blessing and in some areas the nobility retained its power. Autocrats were replaced not by representative government, but by other imposed foreign despots. Religious toleration did not appear everywhere.

You must then consider the terrible cost of Napoleon's rule. Include the financial exactions, economic exploitation by France, the impact of the Continental System and rigorous conscription which led to terrible losses in Spain and Russia. Mention also the repressive measures that supported the new regimes.

The balance would appear to be against Napoleon, but you must bear in mind the unenlightened nature of the regimes that he overthrew. A conclusion that summarises the body of the essay and makes an honest attempt to show the positive and negative side of his rule before coming down on one side should get a good mark.

6. 'Napoleon's victories had more to do with the weakness of his enemies than with his own strengths.' Do you agree?

This is a clear two-sided question for which you will need thorough and detailed knowledge, particularly of the period 1805–1807.

You could structure your answer in one of two ways. You could divide the essay into two parts, with the first half discussing allied incompetence and disadvantages and the second half dealing with Napoleon's strengths, and then draw both together for comparison at the end. Alternatively, you could deal with it thematically by having paragraphs that compare Napoleon and his enemies through command, tactics, social, diplomatic and political factors.

Whichever approach you adopt you should conclude that while the allies did indeed have debilitating weaknesses, Napoleon also had decisive strengths, and both contributed to each other, making it virtually impossible to separate the two.

What the examiner doesn't want

There are two common extremes which you must avoid:

1. Everything you know about the subject regardless of the question.
2. Interpretation or argument which completely lacks factual support.

What the examiner does want

A clear structure which includes:

1. An introduction which shows a broad awareness of the issues and possible interpretations involved in any question without making premature assertions.
2. An essay divided into clear paragraphs. Each paragraph should make a different point or cover a different area of the debate, and should be supported by concise evidence.
3. A strong conclusion which is based only on the contents of the essay, and brings together the points made in the body of the essay in order to address the issues raised in the introduction.

You may not be able to give an emphatic answer to every question, simply because historical questions don't always have a clear answer, but you must show the ability to give a thorough consideration based on known evidence.

Napoleon the man

The one enduring feature of Napoleon's life was his ever-present sense of his own destiny. By this he meant his quest for military glory and conquest. He constantly worried not only about his image as a living ruler and military commander, but also about how future generations would view him. He was convinced that he was set apart from other men in the great role that history had set aside for him. This obsession drove him to his greatest achievements, but it also eventually detached him from reality.

He was a bundle of nervous energy and could handle a phenomenal workload. He would often work through the night, exhausting a series of secretaries by his ability to dictate a number of letters simultaneously. On campaign he had the ability to sleep for a few minutes at a time and then wake refreshed.

His obsession with work left him little time to enjoy the fruits of his achievement. His meals were usually very plain and were eaten in a great hurry. He rarely took time to relax and only occasionally would he go hunting or play cards (at which he would invariably cheat).

Like all human beings, he was full of contradictions. He despised superstition, but he believed in fate. He could be loyal to old associates, often promoting them to positions beyond their ability, but was harsh with his own family. He could be tender, crying openly over the death of an old comrade, but he could also be very brutal, ordering the execution of 2000 unarmed Turkish prisoners in Syria, for example, or the judicial murder of the Duc d'Enghien.

Final Review

It is only too easy to accept that Napoleon Bonaparte dominated the history of France and Europe by force of his unique personality and extraordinary personal gifts. In the simple version of our story, everything can be explained by the uniqueness of the man himself; his rise to power against all the odds; his dominance of an entire country and conquest of a continent; and the great disaster of his collapse. Yet the simplicity of such personal interpretations only serves to disguise a much more complex reality in which Napoleon was the creature of great forces and unusual circumstances which he could sometimes use but never completely control.

His rise to power is indeed an incredible story. How could an outsider of such relatively humble origins advance through the ranks of an army to seize complete power over a whole nation? The story is far from unique. It has happened many times in our own century. Governments often find themselves overthrown by ambitious soldiers who have apparently came from nowhere. While Napoleon may have some personal similarities with inter-war European dictators or military strongmen of the developing world, this does not mean that either they or he were possessed of gifts which set them apart from other men. It seems much more worthwhile to point out the broadly similar circumstances which many dictators have exploited.

Most dictators have risen during times of economic uncertainty in countries with a weak parliamentary tradition. This was the case with Napoleon. The Directory was in a state of economic and administrative chaos and, although improvements were being made, the benefits of parliamentary government were no longer evident to the disillusioned population at large which was no longer willing to act in the government's defence. In such circumstances, politicians are often willing to rely on the army to enforce their will. Napoleon happened to be the soldier who was in the best position to benefit from this situation.

Once in power, it was obvious that the new First Consul was not a profound political thinker, nor was he in any way an idealist. He approached each problem from a purely practical and pragmatic point of view. If concessions or reforms would help to ease discontent and could be made without threatening his own personal power, then he was happy to claim them as evidence of his enduring attachment to the Revolution. He understood only the material side of the Revolution, however, and his reforms, whether in regard to the churches, banks or schools, all had a practical purpose.

In a France that still bore the scars of revolutionary upheaval, he realised that he had to appear to be all things to all men. He therefore sought to heal many of the divisions by concessions to aggrieved groups such as the church and the nobility; but where such groups could not be pacified, he could be ruthless. His treatment of the remaining Jacobins after 1799 is evidence not only of the deep suspicion and contempt in which he held political thinkers, but also of a noticeable drift to the right during his reign. As he grew older his regime appeared more authoritarian. He became increasingly enamoured with the returning aristocracy and favoured them for official appointments. It became more and more difficult to rise through the ranks of the army or the civil service as a clique of individuals began to feel settled and confident in his patronage. However much one may question his relationship to the Revolution, there is no doubt that as his reign progressed he became more and more conservative.

His conquest of Europe has been explained elsewhere in this book as the triumph of a more advanced society over backward rivals. It would be absurd completely to ignore Napoleon's personal contribution to the victories of 1805–1807 and simply list them all as a belated result of the Revolution. Yet, when we consider the military talents that Napoleon possessed, we see that he was as much a product of France's revolutionary past as the new armies or the enthusiasm that drove them. He did not incarnate a fully formed genius.

A similar personality-obsessed picture of Napoleon's downfall can also obscure realities. The grandeur of his achievement and the suddenness of his fall have led to images of him as a tragic hero undone by the fatal flaw of over-ambition. Such an interpretation suggests that Napoleon was victorious by 1808 when in actual fact he had merely won the first round of a much more lengthy contest. The Empire that he created was never stable. It had implacable enemies who had yet to be eliminated. Until these enemies could be dealt with, the Empire remained more like a temporary armed camp than a settled political entity.

Napoleon and women

Because, at various times, women played a prominent role in the Revolution, it might have seemed that French women were to lead the way in improving the status of women. It was not to be, however, for Napoleon regarded any advance in the status of women as a real threat to what he regarded as the natural order. Historians have ascribed his attitude to various factors, such as his macho Corsican upbringing, the masculine military environment and Josephine's obvious faithlessness.

Whatever its cause, he left no one in any doubt of his opinions. When asked by a female intellectual, 'Who do you consider to be the most successful woman of all time?' he replied, 'The one who had the most children.' He retained this view until the end of his life. In 1817 he wrote, 'In France, women are thought of too highly. They should not be regarded as equal to men. In reality, they are nothing more than machines for producing children. Society would become upset if women were allowed independence. To depend on men is their rightful position.'

He believed that religious instruction would be helpful in controlling women. In 1807 he wrote, 'What we must ask of education is not that girls should think, but that they should believe ... Care must be taken not to let them see Latin or any other foreign language.'

Who were the Bonapartists?

The simple answer would seem to be the people whom he rewarded. Yet the marshals and top administrators who rose to fabulous wealth and prestige during his reign showed no obvious loyalty when he fell. It seemed that the more he rewarded them the more inclined they were to become obsessed with their own self-preservation, regardless of the needs of their Emperor. Like many Frenchmen of the time, they were attached to the benefits that Napoleon brought, but not to the man himself.

Perhaps the most genuine and selfless Bonapartists were to be found in the rank-and-file of the army. The French component of the Grand Army spent much of its time outside France and became detached from the society that bore it. It became a military club with its own distinct traditions and music. Napoleon was revered by many of these old soldiers who, for years afterwards, kept the legend alive when it was neither fashionable nor politically safe to do so.

The most surprising thing about Napoleon is just how little altruistic support he possessed in French society as a whole.

While Napoleon exploited the peoples of his Empire in the search for the elusive final victory over Britain and Russia which would end the hopes of all his other enemies, the balance was already tilting against him. His victims refused to accept the decision of the wars of 1805–1807, working hard to close the military gap between their armies and the French. With their success, Napoleon lost his advantage and became deeply vulnerable after 1812.

The lasting impact of Napoleon on Europe remains a matter of dispute. After his death, he apparently faded away into myth. He left behind no dynasty with an obvious chance of success and no significant group of supporters with a clear agenda. Even his desire to be known as 'Napoleon the Great' came to nothing. Yet the life and career of Napoleon retains a relevance that makes it worthy of study, for during his time we begin to see the forces that later shaped, and continue to shape, our world. His era provides us not only with the prototype for modern dictatorship, but also with glimpses of some issues yet to be addressed in our century.

Through your study of Napoleon, you have gained important skills for life and employment. You should have achieved clarity of thought. In the case of Napoleon, this is especially relevant because, before you can get anywhere near a realistic picture of the man himself, you must cut through the thick mist of legend and popular image that surrounds him.

You should have learned to be precise, dispensing with unhelpful generalisations to focus your investigations only on matters that are relevant to your purpose. Good research does not begin with

Napoleon and the middle class

A popular theory among left-wing historians is that Napoleon was the creature of the middle class. The Revolution had benefited this group, but it had also raised the hopes and aspirations of the urban lower classes. In order to avoid sharing these benefits, the middle class willed Napoleon into existence. He in turn guaranteed many of their gains while suppressing any lower-class moves towards broader democracy.

There may be something in this theory, but for the middle class Napoleon was not a complete blessing. He obviously restored order (for some historians a euphemism for middle-class privilege), but he also introduced repressive measures which made an impact well beyond urban workers.

In material terms the picture is equally mixed. Napoleon did not have the vision to foresee the significance of industry, and his regime was not really concerned with the development of capitalism. His 'France First' policy allowed some merchants and manufacturers to benefit at the expense of others in Europe, but his Continental System ruined many as well. The growth in the machinery of state undoubtedly offered employment opportunities for many young men of talent, but censorship of newspapers and the arts probably frustrated numerous artistic and political careers.

preconceived ideas, but it does start with well-formulated questions. You should now be able to ask the right questions. You should also have learned how to go about finding the answers. You should know where to look and what to ask for if you cannot find what you want. Above all, you should be able to identify relevant information from as wide a variety of sources and media as possible.

You must be able to analyse what you have discovered. You now know that you can't accept an interpretation simply because it is in print or on television. You must compare information between sources, be able to communicate your own ideas, and consider the opinions of others very carefully before coming to a conclusion. Even when you do arrive at your own conclusion, you must be prepared to accept that this is not the end of the process. It is merely a stage in an ongoing development. You must be prepared to change your opinions in the light of new findings.

Above all, you must be able to empathise with the individuals and groups who shape history. The easiest and worst mistake that students make is to apply their own modern value system to historical situations where they are simply not relevant. You must be able to sense what for that time would be normal, unusual – or downright anachronistic. People can only be judged by the standards of the times in which they lived, so try not to condemn. Remember, people in history act out of self-interest or conviction, they rarely (if ever) act out of a conscious desire to do evil. The end result may not be what you regard as desirable, but before you can really consider their actions you have to know 'where they are coming from'.

Napoleon rises from the dead in this fanciful French painting from the 1820s. Representatives of the four allied powers look on in understandable horror.

Napoleon, the workers and the peasants

Throughout his reign, Napoleon feared the Jacobin tendencies of the urban workers. The *livret* and the anti-combination laws were manifestations of this fear which showed itself in a clear bias towards employers.

Despite this, most workers fared well during this time. Those who weren't conscripted could command high wages, made more valuable by the government's price controls on bread. This may have been sufficient to stave off trouble in the towns, but it never made the workers into Bonapartists. In so far as they had conscious political opinions, artisans were still Jacobin at heart.

Napoleon can claim the credit for finally establishing the peasants' right to the land they gained during the Revolution. This, together with more effective policing, made rural life more secure. The years up to 1812 saw several bumper harvests, and this meant that many peasants were to look back on Napoleon's reign as a golden era.

Against this, however, must be placed the enormous burden of conscription which caused resentment and unrest in later years. In the south and the west of the country, many peasants retained their traditional loyalties to the church and the Bourbons, while Napoleon probably gained nothing more than passive support from the rest.

Index